PRESENT
MOMENT
AWARENESS

PRESENT
MOMENT
AWARENESS

A SIMPLE, STEP-BY-STEP
GUIDE TO LIVING IN THE NOW

SHANNON DUNCAN

NEW WORLD LIBRARY
NOVATO, CALIFORNIA

New World Library
14 Pamaron Way
Novato, CA 94949

Library of Congress Cataloging-in-Publication Data
Duncan, Shannon, 1970–
  Present moment awareness : a simple, step-by-step guide to living in the now / Shannon Duncan.
      p.   cm.
Includes bibliographical references.
  ISBN 1-57731-412-3 (hardcover : alk. paper)
  1. Conduct of life. I. Title.
  BF637.C5 D86 2003
  158.1—dc21   2002153577

ISBN 1-57731-485-9

♻ Printed in Canada on 100% postconsumer waste recycled paper

g A proud member of the Green Press Initiative

Distributed to the trade by Publishers Group West

10   9   8   7   6   5   4   3   2   1

To Madeline, for being my little Buddha

To Taffy, for lighting my path

CONTENTS

PRESENT MOMENT AWARENESS   xi

Focus Tool   xvi

Getting the Most from This Book   xvii
❖ Ponder This: Pondering   xix

THE POWER OF THIS MOMENT   1

Right Here, Right Now   3
❖ Try This: A Glimpse of the Present Moment   4
❖ Ponder This: Using Your Time   6

There Are No Ordinary Moments   7
❖ Try This: Doing Something Ordinary   9
What Was Your Experience?   11

Breathing — Our Anchor in the Now   14
❖ Try This: Anchoring in Your Breath   15
What Was Your Experience?   17

Tension — Numbing Our Experience of Life   18
❖ Try This: Body Scan   18

Detaching from Our Thoughts   22
❖ Try This: Be Aware of Your Thoughts   23
What Was Your Experience?   24
❖ Homework: Staying Present Throughout the Day   26
What Was Your Experience?   27

What Have We Learned?   28

THE ILLUSION OF LIMITATIONS 29

Thoughts As Reality 31

Questioning Beliefs 34

❖ Ponder This: Your Drama 35

❖ Ponder This: Who Are You? 38

❖ Try This: Make a List of the Positive and the Negative 40

Mind Traps 40

❖ Try This: Pick a Color 43

❖ Try This: Pick Another Color 44

Accepting "What Is" 46

❖ Ponder This: Accepting What Is 48

Loosening Your Grip 49

❖ Ponder This: Swim or Drown, It Is Your Choice 51

❖ Ponder This: Hiking 52

❖ Core Exercise: Breaking the Illusion of Limitations 54

❖ Homework: Quiet Time 55

What Have We Learned? 56

EMOTIONAL PRESENCE 57

Emotion: Our Thoughts in Motion 59

❖ Ponder This: The Emotional Compass 61

Out of Control 62

❖ Ponder This: Chasing Your Own Tail 64

Clinging and Aversion 66

❖ Ponder This: Mood Altering 68

Fear of Our Emotions 70

❖ Ponder This: What Really Gets You Going? 74

Inner Space   75
❖ Try This: Emotional Awareness   77
What Was Your Experience?   79
❖ Homework: Observing Emotions   80
What Was Your Experience?   82

What Have We Learned?   86

REACTIVITY ROLLER COASTER   87

Our Formative Years   89

Being a Child   91

Damaging Your Sense of Self   96

False Selves   99

❖ Ponder This: May I See Your Identification, Please?   103

Reactivity   105

❖ Ponder This: Your Reactivity   107

The Way Out Is Through   109

❖ Homework: Quiet Reflective Time   116
What Was Your Experience?   118

What Have We Learned?   124

SOME FINAL WORDS   127

Acknowledgments   133

Sources   135

About the Author   137

PRESENT MOMENT
AWARENESS

If you have picked up this book, then odds are that in some way you feel dissatisfied with your life. You are not alone. Most of us have a gnawing sense that we are missing out on something more. We just can't put our finger on what it is. Many strive to do more, to attain more, to be more, yet we are left feeling empty. What do any of us really want? It usually boils down to the following: to be noticed, understood, respected, and loved. If examined closely, most of our efforts are pointed toward these basic needs. In essence, we want to be valued as human beings. For many of us, our discontent comes from believing, deep down inside, that we aren't.

So what does any of this have to do with present moment awareness? Everything, really. Being present in the moment, you have the opportunity to see beyond what your fears and insecurities tell you and open yourself to a nearly limitless array of new choices. In learning to live in the present, you discover how to set aside emotional baggage from the past, and worries about the future, in order to appreciate the opportunities you have available to you, right here and right now.

can enable you to:

- Stay sharp and focused at work or school
- Cease to pointlessly wrestle with circumstances beyond your control
- Discover your dreams and make them real
- Quit worrying and start living
- Let your real self shine and draw others to you
- Improve your relationships
- Be a better parent
- Do work you enjoy and enjoy your work
- Improve communication with others
- Experience the joy that comes from living fully

The primary requirements for success in this effort are intent and honesty. If you sincerely intend to be honest with yourself and make positive changes wherever you feel it is pertinent, then you have the ability to grow and attain the happiness you've been searching for.

Does this seem too good to be true? It isn't! With heart-felt time and effort, these positive changes in your life can begin to happen naturally. Learning to live in the present moment brings about a shift in our perception, rather than a mere change in our behavior. This is an incredibly powerful and life-altering experience. Remember when you first realized your sexuality? In one fell swoop, your thoughts and behavior pertaining to nearly every aspect of your life changed for all time. This is the same principle — when your perspective on life shifts, changes in your feelings and behavior will naturally follow suit. Your life can become less of a struggle and more of a pleasure when you learn what it means to be present in the moment.

There are **four phases** to this process; each is a chapter in this book:

1. THE POWER OF THIS MOMENT

The first phase is becoming aware of the present moment through "being" in our body. Learning to pay attention to our senses is the crucial first step in learning to experience the present moment as opposed to being lost in daydreams or worries. We will hopefully come away from this section with a solid grasp on what it really means to be present in the moment.

2. THE ILLUSION OF LIMITATIONS

The second phase is exploring the ways in which our very own thoughts can limit our choices and effectively eliminate opportunities, leaving us frustrated, fearful, and feeling powerless to manifest our dreams. The goal of this section is to begin questioning our own self-limiting beliefs.

3. EMOTIONAL PRESENCE

The third phase is learning to be present with our emotions. We will explore the idea that our emotions do not have to be an overwhelming or all-consuming force, even though for many of us they are exactly that. Learning to experience our emotions in the present moment is gaining the ability to not let what we feel overwhelm and ultimately control us.

4. REACTIVITY ROLLER COASTER

The fourth and final phase is being present with our emotional reactivity and discovering the origins of our discontent. As we will learn, our reactivity is one of the primary reasons we do not live in the present moment and therefore suffer in our lives.

FOCUS TOOL

A "Focus Tool" is simply something a person can use to help remind them to practice living in the moment. It is easy to relax in a favorite chair, read a book, and nod in agreement with what we are reading. It is something else to actually take those concepts and apply them during the stresses of our everyday lives. The Focus Tool acts as a waking alarm clock, a reminder to be aware of the life happening all around us and to participate in it. Ve simply, the Focus Tool repeatedly reminds us to stop anc smell the roses. Within the framework of this book, it is to be used while practicing the exercises until the application of the principles becomes second nature. I offer a specially designed Focus Tool in the back of this book. This compact electronic device alerts you randomly throughout your day to bring your attention back to the present. However, telephones, pagers, cell phones, car alarms, doorbells, flashing lights, etc., can all serve as Focus Tools, reminders to bring ourselves out of our daydreams and back into the present.

Little else needs to be said about the Focus Tool other than to use it. The kind of awareness we hope to encourage can become a permanent change in how we live. Because it takes some perseverance in the beginning, we should not hesitate to rely on the Focus Tool continuously when practicing the exercises in this book. With sincere intentions for positive change and a little effort, we will eventually begin to find ourselves already in the moment each time the tool alerts us.

GETTING THE MOST FROM THIS BOOK

This book, while making a lot of statements, is really a book of questions. After reading each topic, stop and ask yourself how it might apply to your own life. To find _w answers, we must first open ourselves to new questions. Even if nothing comes to mind right away, you might be surprised at what will occur to you later because you took a little time to ponder what you read.

This material becomes even more useful by simply paying attention to how you feel about everything you read. By observing what emotions and reactions are stirred up as you are reading, or later pondering what you've read, you can gain a great deal of insight into yourself. Becoming anxious or frustrated while reading is a great indicator that our buttons are being pushed. Instead of allowing these feelings to stop your progress, simply accept them as indicators that you are moving in the right direction. Sometimes, truly, the only way out of the dissatisfaction we have with our lives is to pass right through it.

This book contains three different kinds of exercises. They are "Try This," "Ponder This," and "Homework." It is important to do the "Try This" and "Ponder This" exercises as you read them because understanding their concepts is important to understanding the overall ideas being presented. You should perform the "Homework" exercises throughout each day in an effort to apply the concepts being taught and to learn what it means to be present in the moment.

❖ PONDER THIS ❖
Pondering

Each "Ponder This" exercise should be contemplated quietly. This doesn't really mean *thinking*, but rather a quiet mulling over. As you ponder, you should sit or lie quietly in a relaxed and comfortable position and, for at least a few moments, let your tension and worries go and simply consider the idea that has been presented or the questions that have been asked. You don't need to reach any real conclusions necessarily; you only need to consider the ideas within the context of your own life and experiences.

Imagine possessing a level of knowing, relaxed confidence that illuminates your path through life with amazing clarity. Try to envision a state of being that is not influenced by the burden of past pain or the worry of an uncertain future. This pursuit begins and ends in our awareness of the present moment. But these ideas do require an open mind. You can always decide later that all of this Present Moment Awareness stuff is a bunch of garbage and that you don't believe it will help you. For now just keep an open mind and give it a whirl. You have nothing to lose and everything to gain!

With that being said, why don't we begin? After all, there is no time like the present...

THE POWER
OF THIS
MOMENT

He is blessed over all mortals
who loses no moment of the passing life
in remembering the past.

— Henry David Thoreau

I never think of the future.
It comes soon enough.

—– Albert Einstein

L iving in the present moment is the full awareness and appreciation of the life we have, right here and right now. Present moment awareness is being aware of what is happening in ourselves and our world instead of being lost in random fears from the past and uncertainties, hopes, and expectations for the future. In the absence of those fantasies we have the opportunity to enjoy our day-to-day living.

To get started, we need to gain a sense of what it feels like to be present. The ideas and exercises in this first section may seem simplistic, but they are crucial to understanding the deeper concepts that come later in the book. Like the layers of an onion, we are peeling away the causes of our discontent, starting with the most easily recognized symptoms.

RIGHT HERE, RIGHT NOW

When we are living in the present moment, we are using our bodies for the purpose for which they were designed — to feel the raw, uncontaminated reality of life. By learning to be deeply aware of our physical senses, our thoughts, and our emotions, we can greatly increase the clarity of that experience. In making this effort to be present with ourselves, we are fostering the opportunity to grow.

Most of us carry a great deal of fear over what is yet to come, which leads us to react blindly to the inevitable obstacles that appear from time to time in our lives. In being so absorbed in our worries, we miss out on the only real life we have — the one happening right here and right now in the present moment. Because so many of us are not used to simply "being" with ourselves, without some kind of distraction, it is not uncommon to find the barriers of anxiousness or restlessness blocking our way. This is completely normal and should not be allowed to distract or dissuade us from our efforts here. As we shall explore later, these can be some of the greatest inhibitors to the enjoyment of our lives.

❖ TRY THIS ❖

A Glimpse of the Present Moment

When we are present in the moment, we are not thinking about our environment. We are simply experiencing it. The goal is to observe without judgment, analysis, or thought.

Take some time to notice what you are experiencing in this moment. To do this you should pay attention to all of your senses. What is the temperature? How bright is the lighting? Are your hands cold? Feet warm? What do you smell? Do you notice random thoughts floating through your mind? Are you feeling any specific emotions? Are you relaxed or tense? How does it feel to be supported by your chair? How does this book feel in your hands? What sounds can you hear?

For example, if your cat's litter box is a little rank, don't consume yourself with thoughts of changing it. Simply experience the smell "as it is," and allow any thought of changing the litter to float by. Notice how you can be aware of something, such as a stinky litter box, without having to conduct a mental dialog about it. You can be aware of what needs to be done without having to think about it. This excess thinking is mental static, a noise in your mind that distracts you from the reality of the present moment.

Close the book now and take this opportunity to glimpse the present moment. When you feel comfortable with this exercise, please continue.

❖ ❖

Welcome back. In doing this exercise, you may have experienced a few moments of being present in the here and now. Usually most of us only become truly present during moments of breathtaking beauty that defy analysis. An amazing sunset or holding a newborn baby can leave us in awed silence as we simply absorb the experience. Our efforts here are to become aware of how often we allow ourselves to become absorbed in mental static instead of appreciating the endless opportunities to really enjoy our lives that present themselves all the time.

During this exercise, you were present if you were aware of yourself and your environment. If you did in fact notice the smell of your cat's litter box, for example, you simply allowed yourself to be aware of it. You then experienced the unpleasant way it affected your sense of smell. Being present means that when the thought to clean it appeared, you simply acknowledged your awareness of the thought and allowed it to float by. If thoughts such as "When am I going to do it?" or "Why haven't I done it yet?" entered your mind, you simply let them pass in and out of your awareness.

❖ PONDER THIS ❖

Using Your Time

This exercise is a simple illustration of your powerful ability to choose and to be at peace with your choices. This exercise is meant to deepen your idea of what it means to be in the moment and to get you thinking in terms of how being present can give you some objective distance from needless worry and negative thoughts.

What was the last task you "beat yourself up" for not doing? How did this thought process make you feel? What if instead of becoming lost in your mental static about it, you had just given yourself three simple choices?

1. Do the task now.
2. Do the task later.
3. Do not do the task.

Could you ever see yourself selecting one of these options and letting it go at that? Can you see how much time and energy you would free up in doing so? How many times a week do you become absorbed in needless mental static about a task?

❖ ❖

THERE ARE NO
ORDINARY MOMENTS

I came up with the idea for the Focus Tool while mowing my lawn. It had become clear through that experience that a tool to periodically remind me to come back into this moment could be very powerful in my quest to live a more joyful and peaceful life.

My pager had gone off several times while I was mowing. The first time, I noticed that I was thinking about getting the oil changed in my car. For a while I paid attention to mowing the lawn and then my mind must have wandered, because the next time it went off, I was planning next week's schedule. To bring myself back, I noticed the smell of freshly cut grass. That's how it went for the rest of the time I was mowing.

When I finished, I realized that every time my pager went off, I was thinking about something that might happen in the future. When I was concentrating on mowing the lawn, I was enjoying the sun, the breeze, the time to myself, the smell of freshly cut grass, the feel of the exercise as it tested my body, and my sense of accomplishment. When I was distracted, I was thinking of things like the fact that I had to take my daughter to the doctor on Monday. I realized that this thought actually made me anxious because she can sometimes carry on in the doctor's office — especially if she needs a shot. My thoughts and anxiety floated away all by themselves each time I was truly in tune with my immediate task and surroundings. I learned that being in the present and paying attention to something as ordinary as mowing the lawn was much more enjoyable than worrying or obsessing about the future.

I realized that much of my anxiety, unhappiness, frustration, and discontent in life stemmed from reliving past experiences or creating new ones in my head. By staying present while doing something as commonplace as mowing the lawn, I saw clearly that I could decrease my inner turbulence. This left me with a sense of peace, allowing me to actually enjoy those ordinary moments I would have otherwise completely missed.

❖   TRY THIS   ❖

Doing Something Ordinary

The previous exercises should have introduced you to what being in the present moment really means. Now, instead of being present while doing nothing, try to be present while carrying out an ordinary activity such as cleaning your home, shopping, eating, or anything else that you do regularly. This is an excellent opportunity to develop your awareness of how we tend to drift off while engaged in habitual activities.

Any simple activity, like brushing your teeth or washing the dishes, will do. During these ordinary tasks, you can easily fade into thought-filled daydreams or worries. Suppose you decide to brush your teeth. You might begin by being aware of picking up the toothbrush and squeezing out toothpaste on the bristles. You might notice how it feels to squeeze the tube of toothpaste or how the brush feels in your hand. Is the floor cold on your feet? How does your body feel supporting your weight as you stand there? How does the toothpaste taste? How does it smell? What does it feel like to brush each of your teeth? If you are washing the dishes, concentrate on the smell of the dish soap or the temperature of the water.

You might try taking a walk. As you do, fully experience the world around you. As you walk, be in touch with your body. Be aware of the weight of your arms as they swing. Notice the feel of the muscles required to walk. Feel your feet hit the ground with each and every step. What temperature is the air? Is there a breeze? Do you smell anything particular? Notice the trees or buildings. Observe the song of a bird, or the texture of the sidewalk. Open your mind to the experience of the present moment.

At some point, you may catch yourself lost in thought. Don't think of it as making a mistake. It is common for people to become frustrated with themselves when they find that they have been drifting off into daydreams. You should remember to always be gentle with yourself. You simply have had an opportunity to deepen your understanding of the difference between being in the moment and letting your mind wander. When you become aware of being out of the moment, you are back in the moment. As you bounce back and forth between being in the moment and being lost in thought, you start to learn what being present in your life means. *To realize when you're not present is to understand what it means to be present.*

You should put the book down now and take some time to do something ordinary while practicing being in the moment. During this exercise set the Focus Tool to intense mode. When it alerts you, you may become aware of yourself being absorbed in thought. If so, gently bring yourself back to being aware.

❖ ❖

WHAT WAS YOUR EXPERIENCE?

I had a good friend, Debbie, try this exercise while brushing her teeth. Here is her experience:

> I can remember that I noticed how the handle of the brush felt and how the tube of toothpaste was cool to the touch. I also paid attention to the mint flavor of the toothpaste. Then my mind drifted and the next thing I was aware of was walking down the hall while brushing my teeth. I realized how I usually walk around when I brush my teeth. I went back to the bathroom and felt uncomfortable while continuing to brush. Then I remembered that my father always criticized how I brushed my teeth when I was young. I just wanted to get away from him watching me. After

that, I finished brushing without feeling so uncomfortable.

When we are present in the moment, we have the opportunity to observe ourselves in our environment in a whole new way. We have the opportunity to see how our past experiences can affect our current behavior. This gives us the ability to move beyond our past to grow in new directions. We also gain the ability to have new experiences we would otherwise miss because we were off in a daydream about this or that.

Another friend, David, tried the exercise by paying attention to himself while driving.

> Usually while driving to work, I would be lost in daydreams or mulling over my immense list of things to be done, but this time I noticed how many subtle things I do. It was rush hour and I discovered how I looked ahead several cars to avoid an accident if everyone were to stop suddenly. I watched the red brake lights work down the line toward me and felt my foot automatically start braking. I never before realized how many beautiful plants and trees surrounded the freeway. It was a lot more interesting than the usual drive, but what's the point?

The point of present moment awareness is to be a participant in life instead of living in a daydream. We do this by learning to stay aware of ourselves and our surroundings, regardless of what else is happening in our lives. When we learn to stay present while doing ordinary everyday tasks, we strengthen our ability to stay present during more stressful or emotionally charged times. Stick with it. You'll be glad you did!

The next time he did the exercise, David was driving home from work.

> I was practicing staying in the moment when my mind wandered to events at work. I thought about how my supervisor had called a particularly useless and time-wasting meeting. Sometimes I get so frustrated with him. As I pulled myself back into the moment, I noticed that I was gripping the steering wheel and clenching my teeth. I realized that hours later I was still tightening myself up over a meeting that only lasted forty minutes. Then I took a few deep breaths and relaxed so that I was able to enjoy the rest of my evening. It seems that one advantage of being in the moment is that I'm learning not to needlessly upset myself with negative thoughts.

Ironically, like David, most of us don't realize the intensity of our distractions until we consciously experience a moment of peace.

BREATHING — OUR ANCHOR IN THE NOW

When we are physically and mentally calm, we have the ability to make choices in our lives. Often when we are losing control, we become tense or emotionally reactive. Not only does being aware of something as simple as breathing tell us a lot about the emotional state of both ourselves and others, it gives us the chance to truly observe how and why we react in a certain way to specific situations. By anchoring in the present moment with our breath, the benefits of being in the moment are complemented by the natural relaxation that occurs with conscious breathing.

When we are relaxed and calm, we tend to breathe deeply from the lower abdomen. When we are anxious, we tend to take shallow breaths from high in our chest and our bodies can become tense and rigid. In this state, those around us will usually tighten up as well because they are subconsciously aware of our tension.

Learning to be aware of our breathing is one of the single best tools we have for keeping a foothold in the present moment. It also helps us refrain from trying to control things with our minds that cannot or do not need to be controlled, a limiting act many of us often engage in.

❖   TRY THIS   ❖
Anchoring in Your Breath

Now that you are becoming more familiar with what it's like to be in the moment versus being absorbed in mental static, you can deepen your practice by developing an awareness of your body as you breathe.

Find a quiet place where you can sit comfortably and relax for a few minutes. To begin, just be.aware of the sensations produced by the act of breathing. Be conscious of the air as it comes in through your nose and goes down your throat to fill your lungs. Notice the sounds of your breathing, no matter how small. How quickly are you breathing? How does your body move with the incoming and outgoing breath?

Staying aware of your breath, notice how much else you can be aware of. What do you hear, see, feel, or smell? Notice how you can be aware of all of this simultaneously without ever losing track of your breathing.

What are you thinking? What emotions are you feeling? Notice the level of activity in your mind. As thoughts bubble up, stay focused on the sensations of breathing. This will help you let those thoughts simply float by once they have been observed. If you notice yourself becoming absorbed in a thought, simply shift your awareness back to your breath.

Notice that when you think about breathing you tend to control it, making it labored and unnatural. You can lose the natural rhythm and it becomes mechanical. When you are simply aware of your breathing, you are a spectator observing it. Remember that it takes practice to breathe normally while being aware of it.

Try this exercise for five to ten minutes. Stay in the present moment as you control your breath. Observe yourself as you deliberately command the breathing process. Force yourself to take deep, easy breaths through your nose into your abdomen. Naturally your chest will be part of the breathing process, but emphasize filling your abdomen with each breath. Breathe in through your nose to the count of four and exhale through your nose to the count of four.

Next, while staying in this watchful mode, again attempt to be aware of your breathing but *without* controlling it. Relax and do your best to simply observe your breath. It can take some time and practice to get good at this, so don't worry if it doesn't come to you right away.

When you feel comfortable working with this exercise, please continue.

❖ ❖

WHAT WAS YOUR EXPERIENCE?

Mary, a friend who read an early version of this book, initially had conflicting feelings about this exercise. At first she counted her breaths, but that soon began to feel like a job. Then she was aware of controlling her breath. When she started to observe herself controlling her breath, she described getting an interesting surprise.

> I had been observing my breath for about five minutes, when I suddenly was "just there." I could feel my breath go in through my nose and fill my lungs. Then it seemed like my chest would collapse and the air would rush out. It was like I wasn't attached to my breathing. It was happening all by itself. For about ten minutes, I felt myself breathing almost like it was someone else who was doing the breathing. Sometimes thoughts came into my mind. I could see them floating by and then out of my awareness. When it was over, I couldn't believe how relaxed and peaceful I felt.

After some practice, Mary was able to experience the unique sensation of being in the moment with her breathing. As a result, she experienced a moment of peace. She wasn't dwelling on the past or worrying about the future. No mental static or beating herself up over anything — she simply *was*. Mary had taken a significant step toward realizing a genuine sense of satisfaction in her life.

TENSION — NUMBING OUR EXPERIENCE OF LIFE

Tension in our bodies numbs other sensations. For many of us, it becomes such a constant presence in our lives that we don't notice how much it dulls our senses and can make us emotionally reactive. It can make the experience of life like touching the petals of a rose with mittens on. When we are tense or stressed out, most of us are far more likely to overreact, or make snap decisions that we will later regret. Simply put, we are exponentially more likely to "lose it" when we are tense. The fact is, most of us carry a great deal of tension and scarcely even realize it.

Reducing tension enables us to experience life more fully because when we are in the moment with our bodies and are able to relax, our other senses become more vibrant. Not only is our vision more colorful, but also physical sensations are more detailed. Sounds are clearer. Smells and tastes are more distinct. In addition, we have more control over our actions and are much more likely to make good choices in our lives.

❖ TRY THIS ❖
Body Scan

This experience builds on the breathing awareness exercises previously introduced. Begin by being aware of your breath and using it as an anchor in the here and now.

Find a quiet place to sit or lie down and relax. Take several deep breaths from deep in your abdomen. Expand the awareness of the present moment to your body by scanning it for any and all sensations. Take enough time to appreciate each feeling. Start with your feet and notice how they feel — literally, how it feels to be alive in your feet. Move your attention to your lower leg and be aware of the sensations you feel there. Next scan the upper leg, then your pelvic region. Watch very carefully for sensations in your abdomen and solar plexus. Be conscious of the muscles of your lower back and acknowledge anything, especially tension. Notice your chest, feel your lungs filling with air and your heart beating. Next, observe your upper back and shoulders. Be aware of your arms, then your hands. Observe the sensations in your neck, and when you become very still, you may even feel your pulse. Note the sensations in your face and scalp.

Take a few minutes to try this before proceeding to the rest of the exercise.

The next step is to learn to recognize tension. Begin by tightening and relaxing your fist. When you tighten your muscles, notice how your hand feels. Be aware of the muscles in your forearm working. Then open your hand and relax. Your muscles should now feel different. Just be aware of that feeling. Notice any warmth or other sensations in your hand. You may be aware of a feeling of heaviness as your hand relaxes. Repeat this process with a few other muscles such as your thigh, calf, face, or shoulders. As you learn the difference between being tense and relaxed, you become more mindful of your body.

Once you are comfortable with identifying tension, feel free to continue.

Now you are ready to do a full body scan. Begin by anchoring yourself in the moment through being aware of your breathing. Feel each part of your body and be aware of how it feels to be alive there.

Notice any sensations you become aware of. As you do this, really notice where you feel tension in your body and where your body is relaxed. Try being very aware of how your body feels where it is tense. As you are breathing in and out, imagine that you are breathing into that tension. Notice how your tension has the opportunity to simply melt away when you accept its presence. If the tension persists, tighten and relax the afflicted muscles a few times and then try breathing into your tension again.

Again, be patient with yourself. Many people have unconsciously carried tension around for years. Just know that any amount of relaxation is a big step in the right direction.

In a quiet and comfortable place, take ten or fifteen minutes to try this exercise. It might be useful to try it with your Focus Tool. As it alerts, or as you become aware of yourself having drifted away into a daydream, take a deep breath and repeat the exercise.

The steps in this exercise are:

- Anchor yourself in the moment on your breath.
- Do a body scan for sensations and tension.
- Relax any tension you find to the best of your ability.
- Be open with all of your senses to the life going on around you.
- Fully accept, don't resist, whatever you sense.
- Be patient and gentle with yourself.

When you feel comfortable with this exercise, please continue. As we shall explore later, tension is usually the result of unresolved emotional situations. When we ignore our tension, we tend only to make it much worse because the reasons we are tense in the first place are never recognized. It is through acknowledging the tension in our bodies that we will give ourselves the opportunity to become relaxed and stay that way for longer periods of time.

❖ ❖

DETACHING FROM OUR THOUGHTS

In learning to observe our thoughts without becoming absorbed in them, we have the opportunity to learn the triggers behind much of our mental static and emotional reactions. This is how we can begin the process of quieting our noisy minds and increasing our enjoyment of life.

Imagine yourself walking along a beautiful beach. The sun is shining down, warming the pristine white sand as the water laps gently against the shore. For as far as you can see in either direction, there is nobody in sight. It is just you and nature.

Now imagine that as you walk you are carrying a laptop computer. It's not that you have any important work to do. It is just a deeply ingrained habit you have to write letters that you'll never send, or create programs that will never be used, or make databases of information that don't really matter.

Instead of enjoying the beauty all around, you ignore it for the pointless processing of information at your fingertips. You might say that you'd never do such a ridiculous thing. But ask yourself this question: Isn't this exactly what we do when we are absorbed in our own thoughts, daydreams, and fantasies?

Many of us have never noticed that we can mentally take a step back and watch our own thoughts as they happen. The problem is that we become so utterly absorbed in our thoughts, as if we were watching a TV show or a movie, that we miss out on the real life happening all around us.

❖   TRY THIS   ❖

Be Aware of Your Thoughts

As in the prior exercises, start by being aware of yourself while sitting quietly. As you sit anchored to your breath in the present moment, noticing your bodily sensations and tension, also notice any thoughts that come to mind. When you pay close attention, you will notice that thoughts seem to bubble up and will then float by if only you don't become absorbed in them. It is a fascinating phenomenon.

Take ten or fifteen minutes to sit in a quiet and comfortable place and practice staying present. It might be useful to try it with the Focus Tool set to intense mode. As it alerts or as you become aware of yourself having been lost in thought, take a deep breath and repeat the exercise.

The steps in this exercise are:

- Anchor yourself in the moment on your breath.

- Do a body scan for sensations and tension.
- Relax any tension you find, to the best of your ability.
- Be open with all of your senses to the life going on around you.
- Observe your thoughts as they float by.
- Fully accept, don't resist, whatever you sense.
- Be patient and gentle with yourself. When you feel comfortable with this exercise, please continue.

❖ ❖

WHAT WAS YOUR EXPERIENCE?

I can remember the first time I fully became aware of my thoughts as happening separately and on their own from "me." I was a teenager in high school, sitting on a hard bench waiting for my turn to see the principal. Assuming that I was yet again in trouble for one thing or another, I was tense and nervous and completely absorbed in scenario after scenario in my mind of how this visit was going to play out. As I watched each scene in my mind, my emotions were triggered as if these things I was daydreaming about were actually taking place. I was sweating and my stomach was in knots when the school bell rang and shook me out of my fantasies. In that moment I realized what I had been doing. I saw very clearly in that instant how I was creating my own suffering by worrying about a situation that I had no knowledge of or control over.

It turned out that the principal only had questions about a sick day I had taken and needed confirmation from my mother. None of the daydreams that had so shaken me had any basis in reality and yet they had taken control of my life just the same. I was fascinated by the idea that something as insubstantial as my daydreams could have the same effect on me as something solid and real. This simple realization changed my life from that point on because my mental static began to have less control over my moment-to-moment emotional state.

We should remember to practice being aware of our thoughts whenever possible. In doing so, we can begin to get a sense of what it feels like to separate ourselves from our thoughts. We begin to see that we don't have to become absorbed in them in order to think. We can plan our day or do our work while still being fully aware of this moment. This is a particularly valuable change we can make, especially in instances when our emotions try to control our actions, such as in situations where we feel anxious, fearful, or angry. We do not need to feel swept away and lose sight of everything else that is happening around us.

❖ HOMEWORK ❖

Staying Present Throughout the Day

In this exercise you will use your Focus Tool to bring yourself back into the moment throughout your day, every day. Through being more aware of yourself, you will find that you can be sharply aware of everything around you. In noticing what you are thinking and how you are carrying your tension, you have the option to take a deep breath and relax. This can make any of your daily activities much more enjoyable.

Rely on your Focus Tool throughout the day. Do a quick body scan every time it alerts you or whenever you become aware of yourself again. Notice where your body is tense and where it is relaxed. Observe your thoughts and any emotions that might be evoked. The steps in this exercise are:

- Anchor yourself in the moment with your breath.
- Do a body scan for sensations and tension.
- Relax any tension you find to the best of your ability.
- Be open with all of your senses to the life going on around you.
- Observe your thoughts as they arise.
- Fully accept, don't resist, whatever you sense.
- Be patient and gentle with yourself.

With practice, this exercise will only take a few seconds. Use this exercise frequently to bring yourself back into the moment. After completing the exercise, try to stay aware of yourself by staying anchored to your breath as you go about your day. Notice how much more in tune you can be to the life that is happening all around you when you are in tune with yourself.

❖ ❖

This homework exercise is also an excellent tool for helping us keep a calm perspective under tough circumstances. Most of us have found that taking a deep breath to collect our thoughts before responding to a difficult situation can help us to keep things in perspective. This expands on that familiar phenomenon.

WHAT WAS YOUR EXPERIENCE?

I had an interesting experience several years ago. I noticed how I would become frustrated when my daughter would become noisy and distract me from my observation of the present moment in meditation. I believed myself to be peaceful and centered and then she would come noisily into the room and my peaceful bubble would pop. I believed that this "disruption" made it very difficult to relax into the present moment.

A dear friend pointed out the obvious to me. My daughter was a part of the present moment. Being present is not about living in a perfectly peaceful and quiet bubble. This would only further isolate us and is actually the exact opposite of true awareness.

Accepting the true reality of any situation is the first step toward gaining the sense of peace that enables us to more fully enjoy our lives.

WHAT HAVE WE LEARNED?

Hopefully you have by now reached a certain level of comfort and understanding with the simple ideas and exercises in this section. You should now understand the importance of reconnecting with your body and your senses and may have gained some experience with this in the exercises. From there, you may have been able to observe your thoughts with a level of detachment you might not have experienced previously. This is very important because it lays the foundation needed to more deeply observe the behaviors and unconscious limitations that can severely limit your potential for happiness.

THE ILLUSION
OF LIMITATIONS

*Getting rid of a delusion makes us wiser
than getting hold of a truth.*

— Ludwig Borne

I n this section, we will explore the nature of the self-imposed limitations that most of us confront during the course of our lives. What is vital to recognize is that aside from the laws of physics, we are only limited by our beliefs. These beliefs, however, can seem as real and insurmountable as the walls of a jail cell. Many of us live our lives confined within a distorted vision of reality, which drastically limits our potential to experience a deep and lasting enjoyment of our lives.

THOUGHTS AS REALITY

The reality of life is that your perceptions —
right or wrong — influence everything else you do.
When you get a proper perspective of your perceptions,
you may be surprised how many other things fall into place.

— Roger Birkman

At one time or another, most of us have become angry and have let those angry feelings loose only to find out that we were mistaken and had no reason to be upset.

We believed that we were absolutely justified in being upset and reacted accordingly. As so often happens, something as fleeting and insubstantial as a thought is accepted as reality without question.

In this same light, we often accept other people's thoughts and opinions as the ultimate truth. Just look at how hurt most of us become if someone is critical of us, our appearance, work, or lifestyle. It is well known that some of Einstein's grade school teachers were convinced that he was at least mildly retarded. Think of the loss that would have been suffered by the entire world if Einstein had allowed those thoughts to become his reality.

. . . our life is what our thoughts make it.
— Marcus Aurelius Antoninus

Furthermore, when we repeatedly have the same experiences, or we have traumatic experiences, our perspective is often stored in our mind as reality. We then carry this notion around in our awareness like a filter through which we view life. When we perceive a similar experience through that filter, our minds invoke an emotional response that prompts us to react. In time we can become like robots, automatically reacting without any awareness of what we are doing at all.

A large dog attacked my friend Julie when she was six years old and throughout her life she has never fully dealt with that trauma. Her early experience has colored her perception of all dogs. It left her to live under the shadow of unreasonable fear despite the reality that most dogs pose no threat. That child's perception of a dog's terrible danger has become a seeming reality for the adult. Julie will respond to even very friendly dogs with feelings of panic and terror at her perceived likelihood of being attacked.

Many people who were abandoned by a parent or have experienced an unfaithful partner in a relationship are often untrusting in future relationships. They perceive the threat of betrayal reoccurring at every moment of uncertainty. The painful experience of being deceived colors their perception so that suspicion becomes a consistent part of their distorted reality. When we approach life with preconceived notions about how things are, we miss out on a great many of the opportunities that life really has to offer.

This is not to say that we shouldn't learn lessons from our past experiences. In fact, one major aspect of present moment awareness is being able to apply the wisdom gained from past experience to a current situation, as opposed to feeling defeated by stress, worry, and anxiety. Developing greater present moment awareness grants us a clear view of the circumstances in our lives, allowing us to rise above our knee-jerk, subconscious reactions. To truly live in the moment opens us to the fact that life does not follow a prewritten script and that to react automatically in the same way to a certain situation each time we are faced with it is to realize the same outcome over and over again.

It is a sign of mental health to question the validity of our own thoughts, which is an acknowledgment of the liquid nature of truth. When our perception of the present is colored by the past, our beliefs are distorting reality.

QUESTIONING BELIEFS

If you don't change your beliefs, your life will be like this forever. Is that good news?
— Dr. Robert Anthony

Most of us have very rigid ideas of who we are and how life is for us; this is our drama. When our view of life is distorted by these narrow perceptions, the freedom and opportunities we have can become very restricted. The majority of us carry an enormous, though widely varied, set of beliefs that colors our perception and drastically affects our lives. Usually, the more traumatic the event(s) that started a belief, the more tenaciously we cling to them. They form our drama about who we believe ourselves to be and how life is for us.

Growing up, I developed the belief that interpersonal connections would always end in pain and loss. I had a single mother who struggled to raise me while dealing with the stress of money and relationship issues of her own. She was often overwhelmed and became either emotionally distant or incredibly angry and frustrated with me at those times. I was left feeling isolated and alone, creating a deeply held belief that I was not wanted, that I was in the way of her happiness, and that there was something wrong with me. Those beliefs put me in the unconscious mode of always ensuring my "safety" and avoiding possible loss by avoiding close relationships with other people. A belief I accepted when I was very young had colored my perceptions and heavily dictated my life well into adulthood.

It wasn't until after I was able to fully acknowledge these limiting beliefs that I was able to begin letting them go. It was scary, because I had to face what I most feared and be open to others. However, facing those fears and overcoming those beliefs has led to friendships that I never before would have believed were possible.

❖ PONDER THIS ❖

Your Drama

Stop for a moment and consider the wide and vast array of potential experiences that you have available in your life. Think about how each new experience you have ever had has opened the door to even more new experiences and opportunities. Now consider the immense range of likes and dislikes, wants and don't wants, can and can't dos, that you carry within you. This largely un-questioned list of beliefs about what is or isn't right or possible for you prevents you from experiencing much of what life has to offer.

Which, if any, of these beliefs would you be willing to question and possibly give up?

❖ ❖

David had an interesting experience in questioning beliefs.

> I was at a new acquaintance's house where he was having a party. There were many people attend-ing, none of whom I knew. As was normal around groups of people I didn't know, I found myself being shy and reserved. I was standing by my-self, lost in thought and feeling very uncomfort-able, when I became aware of being out of the moment. I recognized my discomfort and it im-mediately became apparent how much I believed that I did not fit in.

While doing something as normal as standing in a crowded room, David became aware of an insecurity he had previously not acknowledged or questioned. Feeling like an outsider was so much a part of his personal drama, how he believed himself to be, that he had never even realized he could challenge its validity.

Once David had the opportunity to ponder his discovery, his approach to life was a little different.

About a month later I went to another social gathering. Once again, I hardly knew anyone there, but this time I did things a little differently. Instead of standing off and watching the crowds or hovering around the few people I knew, I started to mingle. Inside I felt very uneasy at first but I knew that this was only based on my old drama of believing that somehow I was not welcome. I started slowly by simply joining into groups, listening to the conversations and laughing at the jokes. I saw that nobody minded that I was there amongst them and that my old beliefs were proving to be untrue. By the end of the evening, I was talking and joking with pretty much everyone. It was one of the best nights I'd had that year.

In challenging his old beliefs, David was beginning to break apart his drama about who he was and open himself up to seeing what else he was capable of.

❖ PONDER THIS ❖
Who Are You?

Ask yourself the following questions:

- What kind of a person do you believe yourself to be?
- Are you good-looking, ugly, or somewhere in the middle?
- Are you too skinny, too fat, or just right?
- Are you smart, dumb, or average?
- Are you a very hard worker, or do you think of yourself as generally unfocused?
- Are you capable of great things, or pretty average in your potential?
- Is life unfair or good to you?
- Are you receiving all that you deserve from life?
- Are people in your life generally trustworthy?
- Do you "fit in" when in social situations or are you an outsider?

Now take a moment and consider this: Any answer you gave was a belief. It was based solely on your perception of yourself and on your drama.

How might your beliefs limit you?

If any of those beliefs were to change, how could that improve your life?

What would it take to begin to let go of those beliefs?

❖ ❖

A driving belief I carried in my teens and into adulthood was that I could somehow obtain something that would make my life better. I became a successful entrepreneur and retired a multimillionaire before the age of thirty. Though I was already well into my own inner work at that time, I can easily look back and clearly see that my driving motivation was still to have something, anything, to bring me happiness. It took having the real ability to buy pretty much anything I wanted to realize that nothing I could buy would provide any lasting satisfaction. This belief was so much a part of how I saw myself that I never previously knew I could question it.

Through being present in the moment with my insecurities, I was able to actually see my beliefs in action and it was nothing short of mind-blowing. To fully realize the impact that my drama had on me was liberating, to say the least. It was as if a dam had been removed from the flow of my life.

❖   TRY THIS   ❖

Make a List of the Positive and the Negative

Make a quick list of five things that you believe are positive about you and five things that you think are negative about you.

Now review the ten items and consider how each list, the positive and negative, could actually be limitations on your potential for happiness.

Is it possible that any of these beliefs might be untrue?

❖ ❖

When we do not question our limiting beliefs, we deny ourselves the ability to effect real, positive change in our lives. This is why, for so many of us, our dreams can seemingly remain out of reach. Cynicism, low self-esteem, anger, jealousy, pride, hypersensitivity, and bitterness are just a few of our jailers. Prisoners of our own self-perceptions, many of us have never realized that we have been holding the key to our freedom all along.

MIND TRAPS

The most dangerous of our prejudices reign in ourselves against ourselves. To dissolve them is a creative act.

— Hugo von Hofmannsthal

He can who thinks he can and he can't who thinks he can't.
This is an inexorable, indisputable law.

— Henry Ford

Mind traps are caused by our limiting beliefs and hold us firmly within our individual dramas. They are the result of our diminished self-perceptions and can affect nearly every aspect of our lives.

My longtime friend Jim's parents were very disapproving and always treated him as if he were stupid. He frequently heard negative comments and criticisms and was never empowered to think on his own. Over time, he came to believe that this is how he really was. He became convinced that he was flawed and unintelligent. He didn't bother studying in school because he was defeated by his beliefs before he even really tried.

Notice the cycle created by this kind of negative self-perception. Mind traps are self-feeding in this way. Because in his heart he did not believe he was capable of doing well, he did not even try. Because he did not try, he failed. Each time he failed an exam or received poor grades he accumulated more "proof" that seemed to speak to the truth of his limiting belief that he was incapable and unintelligent. He was locked in a self-perpetuating cycle.

These types of mind traps often prevent us from experiencing true achievement and are a major cause of the suffering in many of our lives. Just as my insecurities about connecting with other people kept me isolated and alone, Jim's beliefs kept him from doing well in his life until he began to question them. Through being present in the moment with his limiting beliefs, Jim began to break the mind traps that held such power over his life. He began to see that he was much more intelligent and capable than he had previously realized.

A disc jockey in Seattle started a rumor that invaders from space were damaging windshields by using an invisible ray to make small pit marks on them. There was nearly a public panic because drivers started looking at their windshields instead of looking through them — and, to the shock and horror of many, every single one was covered by those suspicious pit marks. To calm people down, sober auto experts were interviewed on the air to point out that the pit marks were always there and the only difference was that people were now looking for them instead of looking through them. As silly as this sounds, most of us live much of our lives in a very similar manner in that we experience what we expect to experience because mind traps distort our perceptions. Living our lives caught in mind traps is like wearing goggles that filter out everything that does not match what our dramas tell us is real.

❖   TRY THIS   ❖

Pick a Color

What is important to learn from this exercise is that we most readily see what we are holding in our awareness, whether it is positive or negative.

Imagine you are driving down the road when somebody mentions that there are more red cars out today than normal. As you look around, you notice red cars everywhere. You may ask yourself, Why are there so many red cars on the freeway today? The answer is that they were always there; you just didn't pay attention to them. The only reason you are paying attention to them now is that they were brought into your awareness.

Now take a moment and walk around a bit. Think about the color blue and then look around you. Notice how anything that is blue seems to stand out in contrast to everything else around it. Now pick a different color. Notice how that color now jumps out at you.

❖   ❖

Driving schools for police officers and bodyguards teach that when someone is skidding or is seconds away from a crash, they should look to where they want to go, not where they do not want to go. The fact is that a person will more often than not steer themselves in the direction they are looking. The negative and limiting beliefs we have about ourselves work the same way; we tend to move toward situations that will support them. The power of keeping an open mind and a positive attitude cannot be denied.

The greatest obstacle we have to changing negative beliefs is the fear that they might be proven to be true. Freedom comes from the recognition that these beliefs are ghosts of the past and have no basis in the reality of the present moment.

❖ TRY THIS ❖

Pick Another Color

Negative beliefs only create our worst fears. As we question our limiting beliefs and break out of our mind traps, we have the chance to see a wealth of new opportunities for enjoyment in our lives.

Just to prove this point, let's try the color exercise again. This time, *don't* think about blue. As you are walking and looking around, *do not* focus on anything blue. Come back to the book when you are ready.

How did it go?

Notice how even though you did not want to see blue, it still jumped out at you in the same way it did when you wanted to see it in the previous exercise. This is an excellent example of how mind traps work. We tend to only see and move toward what we have in our minds, whether it is our worst nightmare or our grandest dream.

❖ ❖

The first step out of these mind traps is to adopt what has been called a "beginner's mind," which means we should question everything, be inquisitive like a child and see everything with new, unclouded eyes. Buddhists call this kind of questioning "the great nagging doubt." It is important to understand, however, that this does not mean we should doubt things pessimistically or cynically. It means we should keep in mind that everything we view as being real is actually subject to interpretation. All of our beliefs about who we are and how life is for us are just that — beliefs. Just as what one person finds completely unpleasant someone else might find very appealing, what one person believes is impossible another will accomplish with relative ease.

We often hear phrases like, "Let go and let God." Many read The Serenity Prayer and may think about how valuable it is to make a positive change without struggling, and yet most people fail to implement these common sayings in their lives. This is because the actual application of these ideas involves a conscious, life-altering shift in perception. And, while these sayings emphasize the value of living in the moment and accepting What Is as the means to discovering balance and peacefulness in life, they do not suggest a specific path to that end. Once we begin to see the world through a mind less clouded with preconceived notions, a universe full of unique possibilities becomes more and more clear.

ACCEPTING "WHAT IS"

Do what you can, with what you have,
where you are.

— Theodore Roosevelt

Letting go of how we wish things were or believe them to be in favor of becoming aware of how things really are is an imperative step toward personal freedom. When we accept What Is we can make choices instead of mindless reactions. We have two basic choices in any situation: continue into the next moment with the current reality or take action to change how things happen next.

It is important to understand how we waste our energies and create an enormous amount of needless stress and suffering in our lives by not accepting What Is. Imagine rushing out the door to an important meeting and spilling coffee down the front of your expensive new suit. To momentarily experience frustration or anger is quite normal, although pointless — the coffee is already spilled! That frustration you feel is a resistance to the reality of that moment.

Not only do we fight against reality in that moment by getting upset, we will usually stay in a bad mood for some time — wasting the precious and fleeting moments of our life. It is a common trait of modern men and women to obsessively wish that the reality of what has already occurred were different. We carry the lead weights of futilely wanting our experiences to have been other than what they were. What makes this so sad is that we then completely miss the life happening right in front of us, in the present moment, while doing it.

My own experience with a business partner was a prime example of not accepting What Is. After several years of being in business, a silent partner came out of the woodwork by entering my offices with an attorney and accountant in tow. He stated that he was not being paid what he was due and that they were there to do an audit of the books. I was simultaneously offended, embarrassed, and incredibly angry as I exploded and refused to give them what they wanted. I felt that while I had nothing to hide, I was *not* going to be dealt with in this heavy-handed manner. In my self-righteous indignation, I kept asking myself, How could he do this to me? For days I was so frustrated and angry that I played out scenario after scenario of what I was going to do, with everything crossing my mind from violence to legal action.

It took some time, but I finally realized that I was pushing up against a brick wall. It hit me that I was wishing that my integrity had not been questioned, my work had not been interrupted, and that the control of the business had not been temporarily ripped from my hands. I saw the reality of how I felt helpless. I believed these people viewed me as dishonest and incapable of doing my job. My angry nonacceptance of the situation was nothing but a desperate attempt to *not feel that way*. Once I settled down with this realization, I was able to calmly show both my partner and his consultants that everything was as it should be, and in the end no harm was done. This was an excellent lesson in accepting What Is. Previously all of my energy was directed into defending my self-esteem from my perceived attackers. As opposed to mindlessly reacting, I was able to take action because I accepted the reality of the situation and I no longer felt helpless and inadequate.

❖ PONDER THIS ❖

Accepting What Is

Accepting What Is gives us freedom and peace of mind. We don't blindly thrash about on an emotional roller coaster that keeps going and going and going.

How often do you find yourself battling the reality of a given situation? Maybe somebody has cut you off on the freeway. Do you get angry? How does that improve your life or change the situation? Instead of automatically getting angry, swearing, and making lots of crazy faces, try simply accepting reality. You can then make a clear decision whether or not this person is dangerous and should be reported to the authorities, or if they simply weren't paying attention. By simply accepting rather than reacting, we understand the reality of our choices. This almost always allows us to make a good decision.

❖ ❖

LOOSENING YOUR GRIP

It's about realizing that there are no problems.
Only situations — to be dealt with in the now,
or to be left alone and accepted as part of the "isness"
of the present moment until they change
or can be dealt with.

— Eckhart Tolle, *The Power of Now*

It is important to understand how we keep ourselves from seeing the world as it really is. We can grip things with our minds much the same way that we can grip things with our hands. Imagine trying to control each individual muscle movement required to walk across a room and pick up a pencil from a table. You would never get there! When we obsess, our minds are madly thrashing about in an attempt to control the outcome of an endeavor. When we are gripping, we are fighting against life in the name of how we want things to be instead of accepting What Is and then making good choices.

Most all of us have, at one time or another, misplaced our keys when we had somewhere important to be. It was like we knew that they were somewhere in the area, but after twenty or thirty minutes or even an hour of increasing panic we still had no conscious idea of where they were. Look at how tense our state of mind can become when we literally try too hard and end up only getting in our own way.

In instances like this, we are thinking too much and our resistance to the reality of the situation only hampers our effectiveness. People commonly attempt to control situations that in reality cannot be controlled by worrying or obsessing over them. This is what it means to "grip" with our mind. When we try to mentally force situations to conform to our ideas and wishes — I want my keys NOW! — we are at best creating suffering for ourselves with our worrying, obsessing, anger, or frustration.

❖   PONDER THIS   ❖

Swim or Drown, It Is Your Choice

When we are worried and obsessed about our future, we drastically limit our ability to make our dreams come true. Imagine swimming in the ocean when you get unexpectedly caught in a rip current that starts pulling you out to sea. When that happens, the instinctive reaction is automatically to fight the current and try to swim to shore. That is when you can exhaust yourself and drown. If you accept the reality of the situation, that the water moving against you is too strong, and swim perpendicular to the current, you are soon clear of the rip current's force and can swim to safety.

Think of the ocean as life. We cannot argue with forces of such awesome power. Like the ocean, much of life moves, changes, and evolves in ways over which we have no influence. In fact, there is very little over which we have any real influence. We have a choice. We can grip our situation and blindly struggle against an insurmountable power. Or we can accept What Is and discover the currents that will move us in the direction that is right for us.

❖ ❖

Notice how memories seem to float up into our awareness in the silent spaces between our thoughts. Look at what happens when we really try to remember something. It is usually almost impossible, but more often than not what we are trying to remember comes to us once we have relaxed and stopped gripping the process. This same principle applies to being creative. Enhanced creativity is a steady benefit of living in the present moment as it too manifests when our mental static is not in the way. When we obsess over something we want, we are severely limiting, if not completely eliminating, our chances for creative inspiration. In the act of gripping we fill our awareness with that thought and block the space required for intuition or inspiration to emerge.

❖ PONDER THIS ❖

Hiking

Imagine you are hiking up a mountain when you encounter a large boulder on the trail. You know that the boulder is between you and the rest of the trail leading to the summit. Do you:

1. Become frustrated and try to push the boulder to the side.

2. Take a deep breath, walk around the boulder, and continue on your hike.
3. Give up and go home.

This may seem like a simple question to answer, but take a moment to consider the following: How often do you react out of anger or frustration and push against the unmovable boulders in your life?

How often do you simply give up, rather than take the time to consider the realistic options you may have to move forward?

How do you handle the obstacles you encounter that stand between yourself and your dreams?

❖ ❖

We all experience fear and frustration from time to time when faced with a problem. The temptation is to wrestle with the obstacle and attempt to bend it to our will. Being in the moment allows us to see the reality of the problem as it is. We can then take a step back, reevaluate, and look for another approach. Instead of focusing our attention on the problem, we should visualize the solution. The problem can then become just another step on the path instead of a mountain to conquer. This approach can help make life, for lack of a better word, *easy.*

❖ CORE EXERCISE ❖

Breaking the Illusion of Limitations

Consider this exercise as the "Core Exercise" for the rest of the book. It covers the essence of what we are truly aware of when we are present. You will be asked to refer back to this exercise several times throughout the book. It may even be helpful to write it down and carry it with you, serving as another kind of Focus Tool every time you open your purse or wallet.

For this exercise, rely on your Focus Tool throughout the day. As it alerts you, do the same exercises that you have been practicing so far, in addition to paying particular attention to any beliefs that may be limiting you. Watch any thoughts forming that start with "I am," "I am not," "I can," "I cannot," "I should," "I should not." *Really examine how you may be limiting yourself.*

The steps in this exercise are:

- Anchor yourself in the moment with your breath.
- Be open with all of your senses to the life going on around you.
- Do a body scan for sensations and tension, accept what you find, and relax to the best of your ability.
- Observe any thoughts and emotions as they arise.

- Notice any limits you are placing on yourself.
- Accept What Is.
- Be patient and gentle with yourself.

❖ ❖

Every case in my life where I have felt discontent and abject loneliness was due to limitations that existed only in my own mind. Until I paused to question my beliefs about the very nature of who I am and why life should be different for me than anyone else, I was isolated and alone. As I began to be more accepting of What Is, my deep sense of dissatisfaction with life began to lessen. For the first time I could ever remember, I felt a sense of peace, and with it a joy in just being alive.

❖ HOMEWORK ❖

Quiet Time

This is a fantastic way to start each day in a relaxed, centered, and aware frame of mind. By applying a little discipline at first, you will find that this quiet time becomes less of a chore and more of a genuine pleasure.

You should set aside some quiet time for yourself *every day*. Choose a quiet place where you can sit upright comfortably. Do the Core Exercise to start or whenever the Focus Tool alerts you or you become aware of yourself having drifted off into thought. Really focus on breathing in and out through your nose, deep into your abdomen, and notice how relaxed you become.

Doing even five minutes is helpful, although working up to thirty minutes or more will bring about the maximum benefit.

❖ ❖

WHAT HAVE WE LEARNED?

By now you should have an idea of how our beliefs can distort our view of reality for as long as we fail to question them. When our perception changes, our thoughts and behavior cannot help but to change accordingly. This type of shift in self-awareness is very powerful, because as we deepen our understanding of who we actually are as opposed to who we believe and thus limit ourselves to be, we begin to manifest a life that we genuinely enjoy living.

EMOTIONAL PRESENCE

Who lives in fear will never be a free man.
— Horace (Quintus Horatius Flaccus)

I n this section we are going to take a look at our emotions. For so many of us, this is important because emotions frequently become an all-consuming force that can severely limit our ability to stay aware in the present moment. In the grip of a powerful emotion, it may seem impossible to see that feeling as anything other than a truth that demands our immediate action. This is because so many of us have become accustomed to seeing them this way. Through developing our ability to stay present with our emotions, they can become less overpowering and we can then have the opportunity to choose how we respond to emotionally intense situations instead of habitually reacting to them. In this way, emotions become our advisors rather than our rulers.

EMOTION: OUR THOUGHTS IN MOTION

What are emotions? In their most basic role, emotions are how our minds prepare our bodies to act based on what we perceive. In essence, emotions are the brawn behind the brain. It is our assessment of a given circumstance that triggers the emotions we feel. An example of this is the fight-or-flight response that is called upon by our mind when we perceive a physical threat.

Fundamentally, emotions result from a biological interaction between our mind and body designed to ensure our survival. Our most basic emotions — happiness, sadness, fear, anger, surprise, and disgust — are intended to guide us in our quest to ensure both our own survival as well as that of the species. They are experienced in our bodies as sensations that are either pleasant or unpleasant. As a result, we instinctively gravitate toward situations that trigger pleasant emotions just as we tend to avoid those that trigger unpleasant ones.

What is important to remember is that emotional responses are triggered by our *perception* of a given situation.

We can feel our emotions in nearly any part of the body as a collection of sensations of varying intensity. Our brain prepares our bodies differently depending on the situation and the action the body may be asked to perform. For example, fear feels different than love, just as sorrow causes sensations that feel completely different than happiness. Rage is a far more demanding feeling than annoyance. Grief and terror can be equally overwhelming, but they manifest themselves in the body completely differently.

❖ PONDER THIS ❖

The Emotional Compass

Too often, we act based on the emotions we are feeling without ever realizing that it is only those physical sensations guiding us and not sound judgment. Take a moment and ponder how often you make decisions or react based on what you are feeling in any given moment. Do you ever gossip or become judgmental of others when you are feeling insecure? Do you ever say things you would not normally say when you become angry or sad? Do you ever lash out at others because you are in a bad mood? In what other ways might you blindly react based on what you are feeling in any given moment?

Think of all the indicators of our society's growing blindness to its own emotional turmoil. What causes the intense road rage that leads to highway violence? What causes two adults to get into a fistfight during a sporting event? Why, when our life is far from threatened, do we behave as if it were? What could induce these desperate acts?

❖ ❖

Even though it may sometimes seem impossible, we always have the ability to choose our actions — regardless of our emotional state. And yet, the vast majority of us have become accustomed to accepting what we feel in any moment as an undeniable indicator of reality. Too often, we simply cater to the demands of our emotions without first questioning their validity.

OUT OF CONTROL

Fear defeats more people than any other
one thing in the world.

— Ralph Waldo Emerson

Anxiety is a thin stream of fear trickling
through the mind. If encouraged, it cuts a channel into
which all other thoughts are drained.

— Arthur Somers Roche

As we have discussed before, how we perceive the world determines our reactions to it. When we begin to question our anxiety-creating perceptions, we begin to expose the beliefs that distort our view of life.

For many of us, it has become nearly impossible to genuinely relax or enjoy our lives. We tend to be continually stressed and anxious, always guarding against threats that might revive our past pains or prevent our future dreams.

Our freedom comes when we realize that most of what we perceive as a threat really isn't. It is when we confuse our wants with our needs that we see things otherwise. *Needs* are what we fundamentally require to ensure our very lives and the continuation of our species. They have been programmed into our brains through the process of evolution. The confusion around *wants* begins when we believe, usually subconsciously, that something is essential to our survival when it really isn't. This can cause emotional reactions that are out of proportion to reality. For most of us, this state of being has become so familiar we scarcely even notice it. There is another way, however. Anxiety does not have to be the driving force in our lives.

Look at the panic invoked by something such as an audit notice from the IRS. You might say, "Of course I'd feel panicked! And with good reason!" This is exactly the point. We have become conditioned into seeing so much in our lives as worthy of a "life or death" reaction, when in reality there is very little to be so fearful of. The bottom line is that while we may all face periodic challenges to our way of life, rarely are our lives actually threatened. In the present moment, those perceived threats are really only circumstances to be dealt with.

Now, this is not to say that we should cast away all our worldly belongings in favor of a good walking stick. Nor is this to say that nothing matters and that we shouldn't try to live well within our modern society. Notice how it is our *reactions* to the inevitable ups and downs we experience that cause dissatisfaction with our lives. Since the ups and downs in life are still going to happen, why go for the unnecessary emotional ride? It ultimately is a choice.

❖ PONDER THIS ❖
Chasing Your Own Tail

Have you ever noticed how the emotions you feel can start a plethora of scenarios in your head? Often, these mental movies are based on the theme of your current emotional state. For example, if you are feeling sad, then your mental movies will revolve around sad situations. If you are frustrated . . . you get the point.

We also play out what we believe will happen in a given situation through these mental movies. For example, if we anticipate being snubbed in a particular social event, then we often daydream about such scenarios before and even while attending the event. If we fear being helpless, then our mental movies will revolve around either being helpless or overcoming helplessness, both of which are ways of mentally dwelling on those underlying feelings. If we are in a relationship and anticipate doing something wrong or not being good enough for the other person . . . again, you get the idea.

At any given time we have a variety of emotions passing through us. They come in waves both subtle and obvious.

When we experience emotions that cannot be readily attributed to something specific, we tend to mentally create fitting situations in our fantasies. For example, we have all woken up on the "wrong side of the bed," in a really crabby mood. We may not have known why we were so grouchy, but we were, just the same. Most of us never noticed how that underlying emotion could stir up all sorts of monologs, dialogs, and scenarios in our minds — all centered around our current emotional theme of feeling frustrated and grouchy.

Can you see how being absorbed in your fantasies would maintain or even amplify your mood?

In what circumstances do you create these kinds of daydreams?

What insecurities do you think might trigger these fantasies?

By being present in the moment, we can acknowledge our emotional state without being swept away into thoughtless reactivity or useless fantasies. This can allow our emotions to pass through us unimpeded and provides the opportunity to understand what it is that actually triggered the emotions to begin with.

❖ ❖

When we can reduce or eliminate our belief-driven emotional turmoil, we eliminate much of our stressful and needless anxiety and begin to gain a real sense of inner peace. This anxiety-born discontent is generated through our tendency to live life according to the principle of clinging and aversion.

CLINGING AND AVERSION

I hope for nothing.
I fear nothing.
I am free.

— Nikos Kazantzakis

Many of us live in an almost constant state of anxiety, yet we are scarcely aware of it. We are *clinging* when we fear that we will not get what we want or that we'll lose what we already have. It is *aversion* when we fear either receiving, or *not* getting rid of, what we do not want to have. This fear lives in the background of our lives and shows itself in our discontent, stress, hypertension, frustration, anxiety, and depression. What we cling to or avoid is all based on our beliefs. When what is happening is contrary to those limiting beliefs, our bodies create an emotional response.

Clinging and aversion generates a constant stream of emotional reactions that can hold incredible power over our lives and keep us locked into our dramas. When we believe that we are a certain kind of person and that life is a certain way for us, we can filter out everything that does not fit within those beliefs. In a way, we become magnetized by our beliefs. We are pulled toward the same kinds of people and we gravitate toward the same kinds of entertainment and distractions. We encounter the same kinds of problems and tend to end up in the same kinds of relationships over and over again. We are pushed and pulled by our emotions toward what we believe will make us happy and away from what we believe will not.

Consider the numerous suicides that occurred after the stock market crash in the late 1920s. Those individuals — most of them formerly wealthy investment bankers, stockbrokers, and corporate executives — simply could not envision a life without wealth or power. So powerful was their aversion to poverty, they saw no option other than death. They had clung to wealth and their ability to earn it because they believed that it defined their self-worth. When the bottom dropped out, they thought that their lives were over.

When we are not maintaining our dramas, anxiety can creep in, creating a helpless and overwhelming feeling, literally making us want to crawl right out of our own skin. Most of us avoid this anxiety by forcefully altering our moods. The vast majority of us employ some method of mood altering to change how we feel — to gain a sense of comfort when we are feeling emotionally uncomfortable. It is a way of hiding. For as long as we continue to avoid a given feeling, we cannot recognize its root cause and free ourselves from it.

❖ PONDER THIS ❖

Mood Altering

Have you noticed how most of us are in a nearly constant search for distraction? Many of us are engaged in a relentless pursuit to become emotionally disconnected from ourselves with one thing or another. Do you or any of the people you know find it difficult to just sit quietly? Most people feel as if they always need to be doing something even if they are not sure what it is.

How do you deal with your anxiety?

Do any of these mood-altering tactics apply to you?

- Work: feeling centered only while working or accomplishing.
- Sex: hiding from uncomfortable feelings through compulsive sexual behavior.
- Television: avoiding discomfort by watching TV for hours on end, every day.
- Drugs or alcohol: escaping uncomfortable emotions through mood-altering drugs.
- Tobacco: using nicotine and the act of smoking to calm yourself.

- Tasks: needing to stay compulsively active with endless tasks or conversations.
- Rage: only feeling okay after venting anxiety and anger inappropriately.
- Exercise: using exercise compulsively as a way to avoid uncomfortable emotions.
- Adrenaline: using risky behavior as a form of mood altering.
- Food: eating compulsively in search of comfort.
- Hoarding: collecting and saving items endlessly.
- Shopping: purchasing an item based on the idea that it will bring comfort, or seeking comfort in the act of buying.
- Cleaning: cleaning endlessly in order to avoid stillness, which might bring anxiety or other uncomfortable emotions.
- Spirituality: becoming absorbed in spiritual or religious ideas as a way of hiding from uncomfortable emotions.

Can you think of any other ways that you or people you know keep from feeling the restlessness of their anxiety?

While these are common methods of mood altering, they are also very obvious. Later we will explore even more common and very subtle ways that we alter our moods.

❖ ❖

It takes no courage or effort to manifest our own worst fears. Many of us simply maintain the same kind of life, rarely stretching out of that drama to see new possibilities and choices. We unthinkingly limit ourselves, so that life feels predictable, familiar, and safe.

FEAR OF OUR EMOTIONS

Nothing is so much to be feared as fear.

— Henry David Thoreau

When emotions cause us to lose control, it is because we are unknowingly applying the principle of clinging and aversion to what we feel. We cling to emotions that feel good and try to avoid those that do not. You might be thinking, "Well, duh!" and you would be right. As a matter of good common sense, we should stay away from painful situations and move toward more pleasurable ones. The problem is that when we resist an emotion — when we don't want to feel what we are feeling, and try not to feel it — we tighten muscles around the areas in our bodies where we feel the emotion. In doing so, we have not halted the emotion, only its natural progression. Unknowingly, we have stopped the process that would have otherwise allowed it to pass through us altogether.

Imagine that someone with a fear of small spaces is riding on a crowded elevator. This person's mind will perceive a sense of danger that produces the feeling of fear in his or her body — a feeling he or she wants to avoid. This resistance of fear and anxiety creates more emotional responses. The person unknowingly amplifies his or her own anxiety by fearing their fear, which creates more anxiety. On and on it goes.

It is the difference between being a bridge over a river of emotions and a dam in the middle of it. Picture our emotions as water that builds in strength and volume against one side of a dam. Eventually, its power can become greater than the ability to hold it back. We will usually find ourselves overwhelmed. This is when we can desert the present moment completely, effectively losing our awareness of ourselves and reality. The pressure on that dam is bodily stored tension. This tension can remain in our bodies for days, weeks, or even years. If the pressure becomes too great and the dam breaks under the tremendous strain, we become consumed with the emotional outpouring. This could be realized as any number of things such as intense sadness, anger, frustration, depression, a panic attack, or even some form of violence. It is the venting of our emotions.

Ultimately, the inability to choose how we will act in the face of our emotions lies in our attempt to avoid feeling them altogether. This is yet another disastrous consequence of clinging and aversion and, ultimately, our refusal to accept What Is. All emotions are an inevitable part of our existence that cannot and will not be denied. If we are feeling an emotion, then there is a reason for it. We can investigate whether or not that reason is based in reality, but what we cannot do is deny that emotion its natural existence. In being present in the moment and allowing emotions to pass through us, we not only reduce their demands on our bodies, but we also gain the opportunity to understand their origins.

Trying to deny what you are feeling is the same as trying to deny your right hand or left ear. Spend some time trying to convince yourself of your right hand's nonexistence and see if it ever goes away. The only difference is that your right hand generally will not become larger and more powerful as an eventual result of your aversion to its existence.

For me, anxiety was always an invisible wall severely limiting my life. If I were required to visit the dentist, for example, my initial pang of uneasiness would rapidly escalate into anxiousness that would lead me to find any excuse not to go. As you can imagine, this made my visits to the dentist infrequent, to say the least. Really, any time my illusion of control within my drama was shattered, I reacted and suffered incredible anxiety.

My friend David spoke about a relationship issue he had with a girlfriend that followed a similar pattern.

> I can remember that when we were out in public she was a real flirt. It was basically harmless and

it wasn't as if there was a threat of cheating or any other impropriety. But in each of those moments I felt an instant hit of intense frustration and anger. Those evenings would almost always end in an argument. We were miserable.

One evening when these same old issues reappeared, with some monumental effort I was able to stay in the moment with those feelings without reacting. When I would start to feel uneasy, I really focused on doing the Core Exercise. I hated feeling so angry and was really tired of fighting.

I went off by myself and sat in a dark and quiet room. It took some time but eventually I could see that anger was not at the heart of what I was feeling. Each time she flirted, I would nosedive into self-pity. I was feeling insecure and honestly believed that I was not good enough for her and that I was going to lose her because of it. Dropping into that place was like dropping into quicksand. It was suffocating and terrifying. My anxiety-driven anger was like an automatic defense protecting me from feeling so helpless and worthless.

It was in that moment that I realized that everything I was feeling was within me. She wasn't making me feel this way; these feelings of insecurity really had nothing to do with her. I realized I was making the choice to be with her, flirting and all. That evening, instead of my accusing her of being a bad person, we talked about how I felt. It made an enormous difference. When I stopped behaving as if I were being attacked, I stopped attacking her in our arguments. For the first time, we were able to stay present and genuinely communicate about this issue in our relationship.

❖   PONDER THIS   ❖
What Really Gets You Going?

We have just explored the idea that our aversion to certain emotions is what causes us to lose control when faced with them. Can you think of any emotions that seem to overwhelm you? Can you narrow the triggers of those emotions down to specific circumstances or types of people? What is so powerful about these circumstances or people that they seemingly force you to give up your ability to choose how you feel or behave?

As we have seen, clinging and aversion can really limit our lives. Beginning to identify circumstances that generate reactive emotions may help you get a sense of their underlying causes. This is how we can begin to reduce our self-imposed limitations, something we shall explore more fully in the next section.

❖ ❖

Although some emotions may seem unpleasant, we must fully embrace and accept all of them if we wish to avoid their control of us. The way out of needless suffering is to fully accept the reality of whatever we are feeling. Through our acceptance of our feelings, we can give ourselves more space. This allows us the room we need to take an objective step back and better see the reality of any situation at hand.

INNER SPACE

When we are not absorbed in emotional turmoil, we are at peace, meaning we are still and quiet inside. The stillness of this space is the essence of inner peace. Whenever we feel overwhelmed by emotions, a shift in perspective becomes our salvation. When we take a step back and feel the still and quiet space that is always within us regardless of whatever else might be going on, we can reduce any emotions we might be feeling to their proper importance. Just remember that we always have more space available within us than any emotional reactivity could ever fill.

When you are present in the moment with any emotional reaction, you have the opportunity to view it from a detached or spectator's viewpoint. Imagine you are playing football. On the field, you are consumed with the images of the other players, the desire to win the game, the fear of being tackled, the strategy of the next play, and the roar of the crowd. Your senses are overwhelmed with the game and you are aware of nothing else. Now imagine that you are a spectator. The immediate urgency of the running play is reduced tenfold. You are able to fully appreciate what is happening with a level of detachment that allows you to not only see and understand the game as it unfolds, but also to be aware of and even engage in other things that may be occurring around you.

The same thing is true with any emotional reactivity. When you are overwhelmed by what you are feeling and compelled to take immediate action, it can occupy your entire awareness, making you blind to everything else. Instead, when you observe and are able to pay attention to your physical sensations, you notice that other things are happening in your body, in your mind, and in the world around you. There is simply more space between you and the emotion. The urgency of what you are feeling is no longer all-consuming. You can begin to get a wider sense of what is actually occurring. With even a modicum of detachment, the overwhelming qualities of the emotional reaction can be brought into a more realistic perspective.

In learning to live in the present moment, we are gaining more control over how we react to the world around us. Instead of being consumed with the desire to act based solely on the influence of any one emotion, we take a moment to see the big picture. With this, we see a wealth of new choices, allowing us more freedom and opportunities.

❖ TRY THIS ❖
Emotional Awareness

This exercise will give you an opportunity to observe your emotions as they occur in your body. When beginning this type of exercise, it is best not to try it while in the middle of an argument or when feeling overwhelmed, because it can be very challenging to achieve the required detachment without some practice. With this in mind, we will begin with a less stressful scenario. By first practicing in more controlled situations, the sheer intensity of our powerful emotions has less opportunity to overwhelm.

To prepare for this exercise, rent a favorite movie that pulls on your heartstrings or evokes strong emotions in you.

While you watch the movie, use the Focus Tool to pull yourself out of the experience so you can observe how your emotions feel in your body. Set your Focus Tool so it will alert you frequently. Then begin watching the movie. When the Focus Tool goes off, or when you feel yourself become aware, put the movie on pause for a few moments and observe yourself. Do the Core Exercise (see page 54) and notice what emotions you are experiencing and how your body feels. Do not feel, however, that you must wait for the Focus Tool. Stop the movie any time you become aware of intense emotion.

Make an observation. Are you sad, resentful, depressed, elated, angry, excited, fearful, or a combination thereof? How does that emotion feel in your body? Notice all of your sensations. Everything about this emotion is contained within you — *you own every aspect and are in control, as long as you remain aware of yourself.* After you have observed your emotions and physical sensations, resume the movie. You may note that when you are intensely waiting for an emotion, it will not happen. You will probably also notice that when you lose yourself in the show, emotions will come in waves.

Each time the Focus Tool goes off, repeat the last exercise. Throughout the movie, you may experience several different emotional states. Notice the similarities and differences between each one as they are reflected in your body. Try to identify the specific location in your body where each emotion begins. If you can do this successfully, you are already prepared for the next exercise.

❖ ❖

WHAT WAS YOUR EXPERIENCE?

Debbie chose the movie *Love Story*. During past viewings, it had made her cry almost uncontrollably. In her report on her experiences, she was surprised at the range of her emotional and physical reactions.

> The first time the Focus Tool went off, the lead characters were experiencing total love for each other. I noticed I was relaxed and happy. There were warm feelings in my chest and it was so beautiful that I was almost crying. I also felt a bit of longing, which created some tightness in my throat.

> Once when the tool went off, she was dying and he was feeling awful. I turned off the movie and I could feel tears streaming down my face. It was surprising to find that I felt bad inside, but it didn't hurt to have tears coming out of my eyes. It was like my eyes were relaxing and letting the tears out. I also noticed that my nose was running.

> Then I felt a lot of tightness and even pain in my chest, around my heart. I thought about the times

in my life when I've lost a loved one, like when
my father died, and the pain in my chest in-
creased. Then when I simply observed the feelings in my chest, I felt better. I wasn't so sad and
the pain in my chest got better. I was still crying,
but it didn't hurt so much. It felt all right to have
a good cry without fighting it.

Debbie's experience is typical. Most of us find that when
we allow any of our emotions to progress naturally, they
flow right through us. We get to see that they do not
pose a threat to our well-being and really are nothing to
fear. With practice in staying present with our emotions,
we can begin to see that we have the opportunity to not
react and gain objectivity regardless of what we are feeling. This is as it should be. We can learn that when we
are present, we have the ability to choose how we will
respond to any circumstance.

❖   HOMEWORK   ❖

Observing Emotions

Now that you have an idea of what it means to be present with your emotions, the best way to continue your
learning is to use your Focus Tool daily. When it alerts
you, practice the Core Exercise, specifically observing
your emotions.

Pay particular attention to potentially stressful situations. Some of these may include calling to resolve a billing error on your phone or credit card bill. Perhaps you have something to return to the mall and have no receipt for the purchase. It may even be a phone call to a parent or other relative who normally makes you very anxious. Try not to plan anything, just be aware of these situations as they occur. This will help put you in the moment from the very beginning, as well as keep you in the moment for longer periods overall.

Direct your awareness to your emotions. What are you feeling? Where are you feeling it? What, if anything, are you reacting to? What exactly are you thinking that stimulates your reaction?

Use your Focus Tool. As you are performing the steps of the Core Exercise, pay particular attention to the following:

Where do you feel the emotions you're experiencing?

Observe the exact sensations you experience.

Observe what this emotional state might compel you to do, if anything — the need to get up and move around, for example, to vent anger at someone, to have a drink.

Throughout the day, experience the degree to which emotions are a part of your body. Make a mental note to watch for a specific emotion that has been particularly difficult to control. When it appears, experience it through its series of physical sensations. You may be surprised at its greatly diminished intensity. Or, you may not. Emotional presence can take some practice before we begin to truly experience less emotional intensity. The important thing is to be patient with yourself, as impatience only leads to more anxiety. Simply do your best to accept whatever you are experiencing. *It is what it is.*

❖ ❖

WHAT WAS YOUR EXPERIENCE?

For most of my life, frustration was easily the hardest emotion for me to objectively observe. During the conflict with my business partner I mentioned earlier, this was especially true. At first the frustration I felt was all-consuming and when I first attempted to be present with it, I felt like my chest was being compressed in a vise. I was tense all over, to the point that many of my muscles ached. I was clenching my teeth and my scalp was pulled tight. My thoughts went over and over the issues at hand as scenario after scenario of what I was going to do about it played through my mind. All of this thinking was invoking more anger and more tension. As I sat there, I was feeling worse by the second.

It took some real effort, but I was able to work through it. For a time, I was only becoming angrier. But as I watched my breathing deep into my abdomen, I began to see the independent physical sensations of my frustration. Instead of allowing myself to be absorbed in my fantasies, I focused on staying present in the moment. It reminded me of driving and focusing on the road so that I wouldn't fall asleep. My thoughts kept tugging at me to drift off, but I stayed focused.

As I observed my emotional turmoil, it occurred to me that I didn't want to let go of my frustration, in a way. It felt like I was giving up, or putting myself at some disadvantage, by not venting what I felt at the person whom I perceived to have caused it. It felt like I had to do something with my emotion instead of simply experiencing it. I was surprised to realize how common this notion is.

I stuck with it and it paid off. As I observed my breathing and my physical sensations, I noticed that there was space around what I was feeling. By being persistent and staying anchored on my breath, my frustration simply released. It was as if all of that tension and inner turmoil simply evaporated. I had surrendered to the natural progression of my emotions instead of resisting them. In doing so, I had not given up on the situation. In staying present in the moment with my emotions, I had actually allowed myself to look at the big picture and make good decisions instead of reacting out of resentment and anger.

Mary, who was working through career concerns, got a great deal out of this exercise. Before the exercise, Mary usually felt overwhelmed by her workload. Afterward, she was able to gain some profound insight into her anxiety.

I was feeling a lot more in control after the first couple exercises, so for this one I decided to face my freelance work. I set my Focus Tool and went into the kitchen to make some breakfast. The very first time the tool went off, I caught myself feeling overwhelmed at the thought of the work I had to do. But I was able to calm down by breathing deeply and observing my thoughts and feelings.

That was when I noticed how much space I really had inside to do my work. Previously, I was only noticing how much work there was to do and would beat myself up over not being ahead of the game. Now I was able to see what I had really accomplished. I realized that I had been making some steady progress. When I took a moment to pull myself out of the list of things to do, I also realized that I spent quite a bit of time worrying rather than doing. I saw that I could actually be accomplishing even more.

I also realized that I wasted a lot of time trying to avoid my anxiousness altogether by finding distractions to occupy my time, rather than facing what I needed to do. I noticed that I felt a strong compulsion to clean my home, or "just take a quick peek" at what was on TV with the promise to myself that I'd start right after. Of course, this never happened. With this thought, I started to beat myself up again, but then suddenly realized that I was defeating the whole value of what I had just learned. After all, it is what it is, right? What is important is what I do right now.

Before, Mary felt as though her tasks were closing in on her. Her worry caused her to lose time and therefore caused more anxiety. She realized that through being present in the moment, she could not only keep a realistic timeline but could also once again enjoy her work. Mary now takes the time to be present while making a methodical schedule. Being present as much as possible throughout the day helps her to enjoy her work and be productive without constant interruptions from her anxiety.

I just feel better at the end of the day. Before, I was so stressed out no matter what I did that I couldn't even start my tasks until I felt near panic. I could never even feel good about anything I actually had done. I think this is the first time in my life that I have not felt totally scattered and behind the eight ball when it comes to work.

WHAT HAVE WE LEARNED?

We must always be aware of the fact that our thoughts and perceptions are not necessarily based on reality, even though the resulting physical sensations of emotion are very much real. When we stay in the present moment with what we are feeling in our bodies as the emotions take place, their power is allowed to run its natural course. The river is allowed to pass, instead of the dam being forced to burst.

We suffer emotional turmoil when we constantly live in conflict with the reality of our situation. This clinging and aversion leaves us living in a place of fearful expectation. We have seen the consequences on both our physical and emotional well-being of not accepting What Is. This is especially true in accepting our emotions, even the very uncomfortable ones.

As we learn to be present in the moment with our emotions, we gain a new freedom to choose our own way in life. We discover more inner space, the extra room we always have within us to step back and honestly evaluate both our current situation and our response to it. Ultimately, we have taken one great step toward a life that is once again our very own.

REACTIVITY
ROLLER COASTER

*Consider how much more you often suffer from
your anger and grief, than from those very things
for which you are angry and grieved.*

— Marcus Aurelius Antoninus

In this section, we will explore how our emotional reactivity causes us to live outside of the present moment. Many of us suffer in an attempt to keep our lives how we believe they are supposed to be. Our constant clinging and aversion causes us to ride a reactivity roller coaster, rarely allowing us a moment of peace. This happens because we have lost our sense of self. When we lose our sense of self, we lose touch with a genuine feeling of who we are and our place in life. This sense is buried under an avalanche of the limiting beliefs that comprise our individual dramas. Letting go of any of those beliefs gets us back to a more authentic sense of who we really are and dramatically reduces our reactivity. Then we can begin living with a sense of inner peace and a wealth of new choices. This is the power of learning to live more fully in the present moment.

OUR FORMATIVE YEARS

What the mother sings to the cradle goes
all the way down to the coffin.
— Henry Ward Beecher

If a child lives with approval,
he learns to live with himself.

— Dorothy Law Nolte

We are instilled with most of our beliefs about who we are and how life is in our infancy and childhood. We are programmed like robots with beliefs that influence our unconscious reactions to the majority of situations we encounter. Reactivity, our unconscious clinging and aversion, is triggered by these beliefs and moves us toward what we have come to believe is "good" and away from what we have come to believe is "bad." Thus our unquestioned beliefs and reactive emotions can control our lives.

For most of us in our early years, the rules for life were modeled again and again, teaching us "right" and "wrong." As children, we began assembling our list of what to cling to and what to avoid based on what others showed us was important and not important, right and wrong, good and bad. Most of us learned that our value as a person comes from our accomplishments, material gains, and how others perceive us. These beliefs came from our circle of influence: parents, family, siblings, teachers, other children, and anyone else who directly affected us. As we grew, our culture began exerting its influence via the media, fashion, magazines, TV, movies, religion, government, and society.

Inappropriate modeling, as well as painful childhood experiences, have created in most people deeply rooted Negative Core Beliefs — beliefs that they are, to some degree, not good enough. They feel a sense of shame about who they are. These experiences do not have to be traumatic or severe to cause problems. In actuality, much of what limits us today has come in very subtle forms, accumulated over many years. But their influence is nonetheless very powerful, as seen in the fact that low self-esteem is one of the top issues treated by therapists and psychiatrists. These Negative Core Beliefs are our conscious and unconscious insecurities.

This is not to say that we should blame anyone in our past who may have hurt us. Holding them responsible for the suffering in our lives today will not change anything. Whatever happened was what it was and cannot be altered. In objectively looking at our past, however, and fully acknowledging what was, we have the opportunity to gain clues into the beliefs that hold us back from truly enjoying our lives today.

BEING A CHILD

*The question isn't "Is it heredity or experience,"
but "How do heredity and experience interact in the
development of an individual?" ...*

*... At birth, the infant's brain is the most undifferentiated
organ in the body. Genes and early experience shape the*

way the neurons connect to one another and thus form the
specialized circuits that give rise to mental processes.
In this way, experiences early in life have a tremendously
important impact on the developing mind.

— Daniel J. Siegel, *The Developing Mind*

As very young children, we did not have the ability to judge our self-worth for ourselves. During this time we were very impressionable and did not yet have the ability to reason. We were simply there in the moment with only our instincts to survive. These told us how to nurse for food as well as how to connect with our primary caregivers. This connection was crucial to our proper development and even our survival. It consisted of our most basic needs, which were to be loved, respected, noticed, and understood.

It is a normal and natural part of development for children below the age of six or seven to be egocentric. At that time everything in their world seems to revolve around them and they take everything personally. How caregivers, siblings, and others in their circle of influence "mirror" them, or reflect back to them their validity and worth, is how children learn to value themselves. If a child's basic connection needs are not met, they often will form a deep sense of shame simply in *having* those instinctual needs, therefore diminishing their sense of self-worth.

Children naturally assume that they are to blame for the behavior of those in their circle of influence, whether it is abusive or not. They believe that whatever happens is both deserved and normal and so automatically take responsibility for their situation. If a child's caregivers cannot mirror them with love and compassion, even when disciplining, then the child might learn that just being their genuine self is unsafe. Anything that caregivers do out of their own anxiety can profoundly influence the child. There are the extremes of neglect and physical, psychological, verbal, or sexual abuse, which can cause a deep tear in the child's sense of self. And there are the subtler nagging, criticisms, insults, spanking, ignoring, and shouting that chip away at a child's self-image. Even harsh looks used to correct behavior can add to the erosion.

Children's minds will automatically develop two basic protections from extreme emotional pain: repression and denial. Repression is a defense mechanism where the mind hides part or all of a painful experience in the unconscious. They generally repress either the memory of what happened or lose touch with the emotions associated with it. Many victims of intense abuse or other trauma have repressed memories.

Denial is when someone sees what is happening but his or her mind refuses to recognize or accept its reality. Recent studies in the world of child psychology by authorities such as Alice Miller, author of *The Drama of the Gifted Child*, strongly suggest that these defense mechanisms are used by far more children far more frequently than most had previously wanted to consider.

What is vital to recognize is that even though memories of painful experiences may have been repressed or denied, those Negative Core Beliefs are still active and exerting control underneath it all. Just as when someone sees something that reminds them of a happy day and they smile at the memory, circumstances can trigger those repressed or denied memories and the original overwhelming emotions as well. Again, repression and denial interrupt the natural flow of emotions, causing unhealthy blockages that can be unknowingly triggered throughout our lives, effectively controlling much of our behavior.

Consider a two-year-old who is screamed at after spilling her orange juice. Overwhelmed by her parent's anger, she is frightened and ashamed. A two-year-old does not know how to handle the shame and the fear of losing her parent's love. To her, those feelings are so terrible as to seem intolerable, so her mind buries them and tries to forget about them. Those emotions, and the thoughts that go with them, become insecurities about her worth as a person, frozen deep within. In time, this two-year-old grows up and her own child spills a glass of orange juice, as children often do. The sight of the orange juice spilling instantly upsets her and brings up old feelings of shame and fear. In not being present with her emotions, those feelings seem once again intolerable and she reacts with anger focused at the helpless child. The parent's rage is reactivity, a form of mood altering unconsciously used to hide from those terrible feelings. As with her mother before her, she vents her painful emotions on the child, reenacting the scenario.

This is not to say that discipline or structure is damaging to children, but it does mean that how children are disciplined is critical in their development and the development of future generations. If a child's caregivers have awareness of themselves in the present moment, they have a greater chance of acting in their child's best interest as opposed to their own immediate need to vent anxiety and frustrations. If they can reflect love and compassion for the human being the child is, no matter what the child does, then the child's *behavior* is called into question, not the *person* the child is. If the caregiver reacts out of anxiety, frustration, or rage, they are unconsciously reacting to their own pain and are unthinkingly projecting it onto their child.

Consider my friend Susan. Growing up she had a good relationship with her father. He was kind, generous, and firm in his convictions. He believed that strong people, who do well in the world, help themselves. He would lavish Susan with praise for figuring things out for herself. When she could not, however, she was met with criticisms and felt ashamed. Now in her mid-thirties, she adamantly refuses to ask for help with directions, ever. For Susan, the unconscious Negative Core Belief that something is wrong with her if she needs help creates immediate anxiety when she is unsure of what to do. She is met with feelings so uncomfortable that she will either work at it to exhaustion or abandon the project altogether. She either gets it perfect on her own or she drops it.

The extent to which a child can be genuinely and deeply hurt, usually unintentionally, by their caregivers has previously been severely underestimated. In fact, many of our current child-rearing customs, which are considered quite normal, are actually very traumatizing to the human psyche. A common example is how many two-year-olds are frequently criticized for being selfish. This is damaging to their sense of self because two-year-olds are supposed to be selfish. It is a completely normal part of their development. When they are criticized for being normal, the only message they get is that there is something wrong with them.

DAMAGING YOUR SENSE OF SELF

Many men and women in our society have such a diminished sense of self that they degrade themselves and abuse their bodies in the delusion that they can increase their self-worth by changing how they look. They have lost touch with any sense of who they are and their value as a human being. They are always searching to get those original connection needs met and can only see themselves in the reflection of another person's approval.

Mary related a story that when she was younger her father would constantly tease her about having a "fat butt just like her mother." It was his way of venting his frustrations toward her. He would make jokes both publicly and privately, inviting laughter (and humiliation for Mary) from anyone present. She was in denial about the situation and to this day insists that her dad was only joking around. She does not make the connection that his behavior led to her firm belief that a "flaw" in her physical appearance lowers her worth as a human being. As a result, this belief has influenced her self-image and her actions for her entire life. Since her pre-teen years, Mary has only worn clothes that hide her shape. She still refuses to go swimming in public places and perpetually experiments with fad and starvation diets. Her belief in her perceived inadequacies spawned a very specific way of life to protect her from the pain of believing that she is flawed and never quite good enough. Like so many of us, her ability to genuinely know and feel her own self-worth has been damaged.

Many children have learned to stifle their own emotions and needs in order to maintain a semblance of love. This brought about the belief that having these feelings was somehow a sign that something was wrong with them. In essence, these children are bending themselves around their parents' needs and anxiety. While this was a mechanism for surviving their childhood, it usually ends up being very limiting in their adult life.

Picture a child who was criticized by his caregivers whenever he was upset. He learned to feel shame for feeling frustration, a very normal emotion for a child. As an adult he distances himself from people or situations that frustrate or anger him, and he avoids confrontation. The arising of those emotions brings with it the anxiety and shame of the unconscious belief that there is something wrong with him for feeling that way. To compensate, he becomes manipulative in order to get the things he wants. After a while, when he cannot avoid it, he will explode to vent his overwhelming rage because there is no middle ground of simply being frustrated and then working through it. This leads to more feelings of shame, which further fuel his sense of inadequacy.

The best description I've ever come across of the phenomenon of a damaged sense of self was that of a bubble, an idea developed by psychologist D.W. Winnicott. Picture a child as a bubble. If the outside (caregiver) pressure is too great or too little, then the child must change from genuinely being themselves to prevent their caregivers from being upset or distant. They learn to compensate, to the best of their ability, in order to adapt to the pressure. Their requirement for basic connection needs is so strong that they literally feel as if they will "pop" out of existence if that connection is completely lost. When a child has taken personally the perceived disconnection from their caregivers, they feel bad about themselves. This is how Negative Core Beliefs are formed. Their not-yet-rational minds automatically and unconsciously start changing themselves from simply being who they genuinely are into what they feel that they are supposed to be in an effort to get those needs met. The more that they are required to compensate, the more their sense of self is damaged.

FALSE SELVES

*Anyone who can handle a needle convincingly
can make us see a thread which is not there.*

— E. H. Gombrich, *Art and Illusion*

*The Beatles exist apart from my Self.
I am not really Beatle George.
Beatle George is like a suit or shirt that I once wore
on occasion and until the end of my life
people may see that shirt and mistake it for me.*

— George Harrison

In our largely unconscious efforts to compensate and have our basic needs met, we create false selves. With false selves, we become like actors in a movie, always pretending to be something we are not. We deny our own feelings, thoughts, and desires as we play the roles we believe we are supposed to, no matter how misguided they may be.

For most of us as children, this was necessary to meet our instinctual need for connection with our caregivers. Most of us, however, continue to use, change, and add new false selves throughout our adult lives. We use them as shields, as a protection against having our Negative Core Beliefs triggered. They are also a way for us to unconsciously continue our efforts to fulfill those unmet childhood needs. For instance, someone who as a child never felt that they were heard or respected, as an adult can forever strive to be respected, often without realizing that this is what they are doing. They may enter relationships or professions where they can be dominant and unconsciously allow themselves to feel that those needs are being met.

My friend Jake grew up with an older brother who was disturbed, destructive, and violent. In order to receive the same attention from his parents that his brother did, he had to be "perfect." He played the role of "the good guy." He was always an "A" student, very well kept, and could not withstand being perceived as anything less. He had learned to base his own self-worth on everyone else's reaction to him. If he believed others were seeing him as anything less than perfect, he would double his efforts to prove himself. If his false self failed, he was met with anxiety that only further fueled his efforts, causing him to either push harder to convince them of his perfection or to distance himself from the "unreasonable" person who could not see his supposed virtues.

In his love relationships, he would also play this role of "the good guy" who always was cool and in control. Over time, when girlfriends started to feel the shallowness of this acting and wanted something more from him, they were met with frustration and criticism. If he could not convince them that they were at fault for how they were feeling, he abandoned the relationship. For Jake, the experience of someone not buying into his false self brought up those old feelings of not being good enough. He once again felt the terrible sting of believing he was an unlovable nobody and unconsciously reacted in an effort to not feel that way.

Playing the role of "nice guy," "people-pleaser," or being a "caretaker" are all common forms of false selves. This is not to say that everyone who is nice, pleasing, or caring is unconsciously being a phony. In some cases, however, people will play these roles because it is how they get their sense of self-worth. Their actions are there for others to see so that they may gain the approval they so desperately need. They've lost touch with any sense of what they really feel or want in their own lives.

If a false self fails to protect us, we can often either have an emotional reaction to reclaim that false self, such as an angry outburst, or we can easily fall into a depression. You could think of depression as a state of being numbed to our emotions, which allows us to continue hiding from our Negative Core Beliefs.

Imagine a little girl who received a great deal of affection and attention when she was all dressed up and cute, as opposed to being ignored or criticized when she was dirty or simply in regular play clothes. In order to feel loved she had learned to play the role of a false self, "the cute one." She grew into a woman who, in order to not feel insecure, had to live life as that false self. It was not that she simply chose her attire and prepared herself in the way she wanted. She felt she had to do this, that it was the role she must play in order to function well in life. A big part of her sense of self-worth comes from others' approving glances or comments. She goes from one diet to the next, and from one shopping spree to the next, in an effort to hide from how she feels deep down inside. As she grows older and fails to get the admiring looks she used to, her false self can no longer be supported, leaving her numb with depression. She cannot consider her value as a human being, because of her Negative Core Belief that she has none.

We can also identify with an idea, thought, goal, opinion, or point of view and turn it into a false self. For instance, look at how many arguments unfold when each side needs to be right and thus loses sight of the real issues to be resolved. They become so identified with their side of the argument that they defend it as if *who they are* is being called into question. Their sense of self-worth is invested in being right. Very often many of us will identify with our imaginings of a different future. We just know that when we are in better shape, have a nicer car, make more money, or get that great job that then we will have more value. The problem with this is that the illusion is broken when we achieve it. As I have mentioned earlier, I thought that having lots of money would finally give me value. For years my goal was to become a multimillionaire and retire young. I just knew that when this happened I would finally be at peace with myself. I could see in my fantasies that I would finally be beyond reproach. It just was not that way. I was still driven to do more, to have more, and to be more. Most importantly, none of my Negative Core Beliefs had changed.

❖ PONDER THIS ❖

May I See Your Identification, Please?

What do you identify with? You might be surprised when you really start looking closely. This requires sincere intent, self-honesty, and a good sense of humor.

Think hard about this question. Who are you?

- Are you your occupation? "I am a consultant, unemployed, a doctor, a lawyer, a cook, a soldier, an administrative assistant, a teacher, a scientist, an accountant."
- Are you your hobbies? "I am a painter, a rock climber, a jogger, a gardener."
- Are you your body? "I am fat, skinny, tall, short, beautiful, ugly."
- Are you your emotions? "I am angry, sad, happy, disgusted, bored."
- Are you your thoughts?
- Are you your causes? "I am pro-life, pro-choice, a Democrat, a Republican, a libertarian, a neo-Nazi, an equal rights activist."
- Are you your ethnicity? "I am African American, Caucasian, Asian."
- Are you a parent? "I am a father, a mother, a good parent, a bad parent."
- Are you what you have? "I drive a Porsche, a BMW, a Chevy." "I am rich, poor, or moderately well off."
- Are you your "good" qualities? "I am helpful, compassionate, intelligent, honest, generous."
- Are you your "bad" qualities? "I am selfish, arrogant, insecure, jealous, mean."
- Are you your achievements? "I am a war

hero, an employee of the year, a self-made multimillionaire."

- Are you your failures? "I am bankrupt, a high-school dropout, an abusive parent."

These things have become a false self when we get our sense of identity and self-worth from them. At that point, they are no longer things we do, have, think, or feel, but rather the basis for how we value ourselves.

Do you think that if any of these things were to change that who you are would change too? Would your value as a human being change as well?

❖ ❖

New choices and opportunities come from recognizing how we use the many subtle forms of our reactivity, dramas, and false selves to protect ourselves from old and painful emotional baggage. *We gain freedom from our discontent and suffering by recognizing that if someone or something can "push our buttons," it is only because our beliefs have provided them with buttons to push.*

REACTIVITY

Our reactivity is an automated defense to protect us from feeling the pain of our Negative Core Beliefs. Normally, we do not recognize that an old and painful memory has been stirred up; we simply feel overwhelmed and automatically react as a defense. We can either shut down what we are feeling by underreacting, overreact with emotions out of proportion to the situation, or we can act out. The person who underreacts unconsciously shuts down his or her emotions to either reduce their intensity or completely hide them. The person who overreacts is unconsciously fighting against the situation in the hope of changing it and releasing him or her from uncomfortable feelings. The person who acts out unconsciously does so to purge their anxious feelings. In any of these cases, when we are being reactive we are completely self-absorbed, which comes from the childlike mind-set stored in repressed or denied memories. We are in the mode of protecting ourselves from our own painful feelings, frequently at the expense of people around us.

Often when we become reactive, we can act self-righteous, grandiose, contemptuous, judgmental, critical, blaming, arrogant, controlling, or tyrannical. The list goes on and on. We can either experience pride when we feel better than others or envious when we feel like less. For the longest time rage was my hiding place. Whenever I unconsciously felt insecure or small, I would become incredibly angry. Just as it happened to me in my childhood, I found myself purging those terrible feelings inside myself at whoever or whatever was triggering those memories. Yelling would instantly relieve some of the pressure I felt and would always be followed with an incredible sense of guilt. Negative Core Beliefs are self-perpetuating in this way.

There are also more extreme forms of protection against being exposed to Negative Core Beliefs, like deviant or criminal behavior and addictions. These can serve as an easily accessed and familiar way to purge the buildup of painful emotions and anxiety invoked by exposed Negative Core Beliefs. Usually, they are followed by feelings of guilt that only further feed these Negative Core Beliefs. Reactive and addictive behavior can take many forms and covering them in detail is outside the scope of this book. The intention here is to show, in very simple terms, how the unresolved issues that created our Negative Core Beliefs often continue to create very real problems and limitations in our lives today.

❖ PONDER THIS ❖

Your Reactivity

In learning to live more fully in the present moment, we begin to recognize that we can respond to situations instead of blindly reacting to them. In responding, we are aware of ourselves, any reactive emotions we might be feeling, and the reality of the situation at hand. It is about making choices instead of reacting.

Ask yourself:

What circumstances can really get you upset or cause you to emotionally shut down?

What specific things can another human being do or say (short of physical harm) in order to immediately frustrate you or hurt your feelings?

What everyday circumstances make you tense, upset, or angry?

How often do you blame others for how you feel?

How often do you have emotional reactions "just because," with no real understanding of why you reacted?

Do you simply accept that this reactivity is part of who you are?

Have you ever questioned the reasoning behind your reactions?

❖ ❖

We must always try to remember that anything we feel is okay and that it is the action we take that counts. We can't always help it if someone hits an insecurity we have and invokes anger, sadness, or some other feeling. But, we do have the opportunity to control how we respond. Our jailer, reactivity, is also our path to freedom. By acknowledging our reactivity and how we maintain our dramas, we have the opportunity to examine, and ultimately let go of, the Negative Core Beliefs that empower them.

THE WAY OUT IS THROUGH

The best way out is through.

— Robert Frost

Our Negative Core Beliefs are charged with unresolved painful emotions. Because there has never been resolution brought to the situations that led to those Negative Core Beliefs, they remain, controlling our lives. When we are forced to face them, they can feel much like quicksand. When we struggle against them it can seem as if we are being suffocated in painful emotions. We can genuinely improve our lives, however, by allowing that stored emotional baggage to complete its journey through us, thus bringing closure to the incidents that caused it. What so many miss is that the only way out of our emotional pain is to pass through it. We must face our fears, pure and simple. Our anxiety around those fears is almost always much worse than facing the fears themselves.

When we can stay in the moment with our reactivity instead of losing control of ourselves, we have the chance to objectively look at the Negative Core Beliefs driving it all. To do this we need to stay present with those painful, anxiety-charged emotions our reactivity has been hiding for us. In doing this, we are often moving against what our instincts scream for us to do. Any time we feel something painful, we instinctively want to move away from it. This is especially true for emotional pain. The key is to simply hold whatever we are feeling in our awareness instead of mentally gripping it through resistance or denial. We need to fully accept that we feel angry, frightened, sad, guilty, or whatever else we might be experiencing. In allowing these emotions to process, we can finally begin to let go of that emotional burden.

As we stay in the moment with our painful emotions and allow them to run their natural course, underlying Negative Core Beliefs can start to emerge. This is not an intellectualizing of the Negative Core Beliefs. It does not always immediately make sense to an adult, because it is based on the perspective of the child who created it. Sometimes Negative Core Beliefs show themselves right away, but usually it takes some time. For most of us, we have spent our whole lives hiding from the way we feel about ourselves. With a little patience we can see dramatic improvements in our lives.

Negative Core Beliefs are experienced as "feelings" until they are named. They are normally summed up in a single word, such as "worthless," "helpless," "hopeless," "weak," "ugly," "small." Sometimes a Negative Core Belief is preverbal, in that it was made before we could understand our world through words. There is no guessing what term will "click" with the belief, but when it happens it is like a light turning on. It is like trying really hard to remember something and then having it "pop" into your awareness. Negative Core Beliefs cannot be "explained away" and until they are experienced and viewed with objectivity they can continue to affect us as they always have.

The moment we describe how a specific Negative Core Belief feels, we have named it. One may say, "I feel small," "I feel vulnerable," "I feel inadequate." Interestingly, once a Negative Core Belief is named, we often realize we have known about it all along. For many of us, we can almost immediately remember having those feelings and thoughts our entire lives. These beliefs often have been so much a part of who we have always seen ourselves to be that we never thought to question them.

Though once we do question them, they can begin to break down. The childlike notions they are built upon cannot be supported in an adult mind. This is where our lives can genuinely begin to change. Most of us have never really questioned our beliefs or the reactivity they create. Once we are aware, it is a lot harder to turn a blind eye to what we are doing. Our mind-traps, fed by our reactivity, can begin to lose their power over us as we start to see the patterns of drama our beliefs create in our lives. The next time we are in a situation that would normally trigger a Negative Core Belief, we have the opportunity to stay present and choose our actions instead of reacting automatically. We can then question those beliefs.

These changes don't usually happen overnight. It takes time and a willingness to face emotions we previously believed too terrible to face. As we have discussed before, this work can be like peeling away the layers of an onion, one layer at a time. With each new layer peeled away, we awaken to our selves and our lives a little more.

David was beginning the exercises in this book when an issue came up that turned out to be a valuable way of applying living in the moment:

> Recently I was involved in a dispute over a local development project. A major chain wanted to build a megastore near where I live and those of us living in the area were up in arms against the project. Richard, the president of the construction company that was going to build the store, is a difficult and unpleasant person

who has a knack for producing instant dislike in those who meet him.

At a public meeting about the project, the local officials did everything possible to silence those opposing the project. At one point Richard shouted in his booming voice that anyone against the project was, "an ignorant fool who didn't care about the needs of the whole community." I was enraged. I walked away from the meeting determined to do something about this and to fight it.

Later at home I was thinking about this messy situation. It wasn't the project that upset me so much as the fact that we were told, "You have nothing to say about this matter and you are powerless to stop it." That made it personal. It was very interesting because I really got caught up in the drama of it all. I was so angry!

Then I would take a moment and focus on my breathing. I did the Core Exercise and took a step back and watched myself being angry. In a few moments my anger started to dissipate and I began to see what was underneath. The first thing that came out was, "You are trying to manipulate me! You're trying to control me!" I stayed present by focusing on my breathing. After a little while, I noticed that I had a very helpless feeling. I said to myself, "I feel helpless," and with this came a great sense of sadness. I just sat there quietly in that sadness. It was kind of scary at first but as I stayed present with those feelings they just seemed to flow through me. Afterward I felt as if a great burden had been lifted off my shoulders.

About a week later I noticed a big difference in how I felt. I was able to choose to take action instead of reacting. When I got involved in the legislative process, even though it was very challenging, I was a lot less angry because I was doing something — gathering signatures, mailing letters, and telephoning people. I was doing something about a situation I didn't like instead of just wishing in frustration that it were different.

This was a wonderful opportunity to experience my reactive emotions in action and see how they affected my life. Before that struggle, I had never let myself feel the helplessness under the anger. This anger had come up again and again in my life and I had never stopped to wonder why.

Our primary goal should be staying present in our lives as much as we possibly can. One benefit is the opportunity to see our own reactivity in action. By staying present with that reactivity, we can begin to untangle the knot of Negative Core Beliefs that can so drastically limit our choices and opportunities. As we diminish those beliefs that distort our views of ourselves, we can once again begin to feel our genuine selves.

In the middle of a tense situation in front of other people might not be the best time to process deeply painful emotions or beliefs. During these times, we can simply allow those feelings to exist without trying to do anything with them. This can be very challenging, but with some practice it becomes easier. Think of these emotions as raindrops on a car's windshield. If we become absorbed in them, then we can't see where we are going or what we are going to crash into. But, if we take a deep breath and look through them, we still know they are there and that there is also the road ahead. Then when we have the privacy, we can really feel into those emotions and examine the Negative Core Beliefs within.

Be aware that early in this practice, sometimes our emotions can intensify instead of diminish as we "grip" our emotions by focusing on them too hard instead of allowing them to simply exist. When we find ourselves feeling even more reactive, we need to give ourselves some space to work through it. Working with reactive emotions requires persistence, because they can seem very tenacious. It can be very hard to begin to let go of anger, fear, guilt, self-pity, and the others because not only are they automatic, they are even comforting in their familiarity.

❖ HOMEWORK ❖
Quiet Reflective Time

Quiet reflective time is when we take some time to ourselves to process whatever is happening in our lives, especially our reactivity. This is not an effort to think about something. It is an effort to relax and allow whatever we are feeling to follow its natural progression. Within those feelings, we can find the gift of a deeper understanding and compassion for ourselves.

To begin, sit or lie down comfortably in a quiet place. Do the Core Exercise beginning with anchoring yourself on your breath by breathing from deep within your abdomen. Do your best not to become absorbed in what you are feeling but rather to observe it as it is. Doing regular body scans can help you not to permit your emotions to become all-consuming. This allows you to keep a better perspective on what you are feeling. Using your Focus Tool can be helpful if you find yourself having a difficult time staying present on your own.

You should try your best to stay present with whatever you are feeling by simply experiencing it, like a curious observer. When thoughts or fantasies come through regarding what you are feeling simply let them float by. Again, keep your attention on what you are feeling the same way you would keep your attention on the road if driving while very tired. No matter how much you might want to drift off, you focus on the road before you.

Whenever the Focus Tool alerts you, or you become aware of yourself again, check in with yourself to see what you are feeling. Simply complete the statement, "I feel _____." As we discussed before, this feeling could be almost anything, and there are no wrong answers. Sometimes these insights will bring with them memories, and other times not. Whatever comes through for you is what is right for you at that time. Stick with this exercise for as long as you can, or until the session feels complete.

When your anxiety is too great for you to sit or lie still through it, then taking a long walk of a half hour or more can be beneficial. As you walk, do your best to stay present. Using your Focus Tool will pull you back into the present. This way you are not further upsetting yourself by drifting off into emotional fantasies. Really pay attention to yourself and your environment. Try to not stay absorbed in your feelings; simply stay aware of them. Pay extra attention to your feet as they hit the ground. Stay anchored on your breath. If your reactive emotions do not open for you on your walk, then you will often find yourself more comfortable and receptive to quiet, reflective time after you return.

❖ ❖

WHAT WAS YOUR EXPERIENCE?

Debbie related a story about working through some of her own drama and reactivity.

> We were leaving for a party one evening when my husband, George, looked at me and said, "That blouse doesn't go with those pants at all."
>
> A rush of frustration and resentment came over me. Instead of giving into it, I took a deep breath and did the core exercises. I stayed in the moment with my resentment. I kept thinking about how he's always criticizing me and how I always end up feeling like I can't do anything right. I was frustrated and uncomfortable but persisted and stayed present with what I was feeling inside.
>
> I went back to the bedroom and started changing into an outfit I knew George liked. While I was doing that I stayed focused on my breath while I paid attention to my thoughts and feelings. I resented George for criticizing me, but I just

noticed how that felt in my body. Mostly I had a sour feeling in my stomach and tight lips. I was thinking that I seem to be doing all right anyway. My job pays well and I have lots of friends, but I never seem to stand up for myself. I thought about going in and confronting George. I wanted to unload years of resentment on him all at once. But as I took many deep and easy breaths and did the Core Exercise I was able to stay with that feeling. Underneath that frustration I was surprised to notice how I felt like a helpless and lonely little girl.

After I changed and George approved of my choices (his choices actually) we went to the party. However, I was quieter than usual because I kept going back to feeling helpless and alone. My body felt weak and my brain felt heavy and slow. In the background I could hear a voice saying, "Can't you get anything right? Use your head for a change." It was my mother's voice.

Over the next week I spent a lot of quiet reflective time by myself in that "little girl" place. Whenever I went back there I was sad and would sometimes even cry. But each time I was able to stay a little longer, those feelings of being weak and worthless began to disperse.

We were leaving for another party and George didn't like my outfit again. I was surprised to hear myself say, "Oh, George, that's just your opinion. Even if these are the ugliest clothes in the world, I chose them and I'm going to wear them." He seemed both surprised and frustrated when he said, "Okay, it's up to you if you look ridiculous."

At the party I got several compliments about my clothes. The most anyone had said to me before was, "You look nice tonight." I realized that George simply had more conservative tastes than I did. I like colorful outfits — not outrageous, just pretty. I knew we were going to disagree more about this, but I also knew I could take care of myself.

By staying in the moment, Debbie uncovered some of her Negative Core Beliefs and began to develop real assertiveness. Her resentment of George's fashion advice was a defense reactivity, a defense against feeling vulnerable and small, which are her Negative Core Beliefs.

A young father and friend of mine, Robert, used Present Moment Awareness to heal his relationship with his daughter:

When my daughter, Sarah, was three years old, her mother and I divorced. I only got visitation rights on weekends and I really looked forward to seeing her. I would pick her up Saturday morning and everything was smiles and fun until the afternoon when I would start to get really frustrated with her running around and making messes. I would raise my voice at her and then feel awful about it.

The problems always seemed to start in the afternoon when Sarah got restless. One particular Saturday, the first time she started running around I yelled at her. The sound of my own voice shocked me and I pulled myself back into the moment to do the Core Exercise and check out how I was feeling.

I felt very frustrated, but I decided to continue to pay attention to the emotions and the sensations in my body. My neck was tight and it felt like my face was swollen and there was a pressure behind my eyes. It was hard to stick with those sensations because I really wanted to let that anger out. I also felt bad that I was angry at my precious little girl and this only made the tension feel worse. It took me a little while to calm down and simply allow those emotions to be.

Through the day I kept reminding myself that it was okay to *feel* anything but that I was responsible for my actions. By this time Sarah was piling pillows in the corner of the room and putting her dolls in the middle of the pile. I thought, "This place is a total mess," and I felt myself getting ready to bark at her again. Instead I went into my bedroom, closed the door, and lay on my bed to have some quiet reflective time and observe my feelings. My stomach and chest were very tight, which felt very uncomfortable. I didn't want to feel the pressure in my chest anymore and the urge to scold Sarah was really strong. To pull myself away from doing that was very hard. It took some time, but as I centered myself on my breath and was aware of the emotion, the pressure in my chest became less intense, and it was easier for me to stay in the moment with my anger. I started to accept that I was mad and that the emotion was all right as long as I didn't vent it at her.

As soon as I really accepted my anger, instead of resisting, it started to fade away. As this happened I became more objective and realized that Sarah wasn't making a real mess and the pillows would be really easy to put away.

As I calmed down, I noticed another feeling emerging: guilt. I started beating up on myself for how I had just felt about my innocent daughter. That was when I realized that the guilt was an emotion just like the anger, and I could be in the moment with it, too.

The guilt caused tightness in my chest and a queasy feeling in my stomach. I was sweating a little bit and thinking bad thoughts about myself. I mean, how could I treat my little girl so badly? What was the matter with me? I felt completely useless as a father. That gave me even more queasy feelings in my stomach, but I just did my best to stay present with the feelings.

After a little while I realized that I could name how I felt. I felt "bad," as if I were a bad person. Then my thoughts drifted to myself as a little boy. I remembered a time when I was playing in a tree and a branch broke. I had landed on my back and my father came out and started screaming at me for destroying the tree. He didn't seem to care that I could hardly breathe and was hurt. All he cared about was that stupid tree. I started crying and saying I was sorry. He made me sit in a chair for an hour without making a sound. I felt really terrible. I had forgotten all about that but can now remember many similar circumstances throughout my childhood. I used to think that he was punishing me for my own good but now can see that he was only projecting his emotional pain onto me.

Now things are much better between Sarah and myself. In only a few months, my reactivity around her has drastically reduced. Now if I find myself becoming overwhelmed, I instantly remember that what I'm feeling is about me and not her. I feel so much better about myself and she is much more open and sharing with me now.

WHAT HAVE WE LEARNED?

From the day we are born, our need for connection with our caregivers is as vital as food to eat and air to breathe. The quality, consistency, and purity of that connection directly affects our sense of self-worth. At the point where we begin to become more independent, any damage to our sense of self shows up in our reactivity and limiting Negative Core Beliefs, which can affect almost every aspect of our lives. Unless we have closure brought to them, we can strive endlessly to get those unmet needs satiated, never accepting that the past is gone forever.

In regaining a more genuine sense of self, we no longer need to get our sense of self-worth from others, as we are not looking to them to fulfill phantom desires from our pasts. We can finally let the past be the past and the future come to us as it will. In not living as false selves, fictional characters for others to appreciate, we no longer feel the drain of playing such roles. There is a lightness, a freedom, and a true joy that comes from feeling our own feelings and thinking our own thoughts. When we are genuinely comfortable and happy with who we are, life is an ever unfolding experience instead of a chore.

SOME FINAL
WORDS

In learning to live in the present moment with my own reactive clinging and aversion, I was able to let go of many of my limiting beliefs and begin to tear down the drama I lived within. As I stayed present with my Negative Core Beliefs instead of hiding from them, I found that I had deeply relaxed. I now flowed through life instead of struggling with it. My compassion for other people, and most importantly myself, has deepened immeasurably as I have learned to appreciate my own value as a human being. In living in the present moment, I have learned that life will always have its ups and downs, its triumphs and tragedies, its good days and bad — but through it all, life is a joy to experience and a gift that I will never again take for granted. For me, living in the present moment has become easier as it has become a way of life. This shift in perspective has opened my eyes to the fact that every day offers new joys, lessons, and opportunities.

In moving forward with a sincere intent, self-honesty, and a good sense of humor, you too can grow in ways you previously might never have considered possible.

You cannot grow, however, if you keep yourself contained within your same old drama. By being willing to let go of those limiting beliefs, you can see incredible benefits in the whole of your life. On this path of self-discovery, it is common to occasionally become discouraged, fearful, or to feel as if you are sliding backward. This is completely normal. Remember that the only way out is through!

Use your Focus Tool and do the Core Exercise throughout the day, every day. As you progress you will begin to find yourself already in the moment more and more frequently. Along with a deepening sense of enjoyment in your life, you will begin to notice new opportunities and choices — this is a sign of the progress you are making.

Occasionally emotions or states of mind may feel like they are too much to handle. It can be very helpful if you have someone who will objectively listen as you talk about these feelings. Other than someone you know, a good counselor or therapist can help with the process of working through these issues. If nobody is available to you, then remember that no emotion you feel can directly harm you. In staying present and allowing the emotion to run its natural course, you will find relief. Ultimately, you are in control, even if what you feel is terrifying. Remember to stay present and allow your emotions to exist, without gripping them. They can and will flow through. Exercise, long walks, or writing in a journal are all excellent ways to work through difficult times, providing that you stay present with your emotions and don't hide from them.

The power of this moment is that all things are possible because you are not limited by your past nor confined by a predefined future. In seeing through the illusions of your limiting beliefs, dramas, and delusions of grandeur, you can stop working so hard to support them and gain a wealth of new choices in how your life will unfold. When you are free from the excessive emotional turmoil caused by clinging and aversion, you can begin to genuinely like who you are and enjoy the life you have. Anything you do beyond that is icing on the cake. The less you feel compelled to be anything other than your authentic self, the more you get to relax and enjoy the ride. Find yourself and you will have already found the contentment and sense of peace you have always been looking for, because staying present in the moment can be easy when you are not filled with regrets and worry.

So take a deep breath and relax.

Your life is waiting for you *now* — in the present moment.

ACKNOWLEDGMENTS

Thanks to Lee Overholster, Ph.D., and Jim Wojtak for their excellent writing guidance.

Thanks to Scott Lipsett, Jennifer Currie, and Jennifer Carter for editing and humoring my grammar.

Thanks to Adam Ring, David Field, Joel Rico, Mom, and all the others who have been patient with me, listened openly to my ideas, and contributed greatly to the creation of this book.

SOURCES

I would like to take a moment to express my sincere appreciation to the following authors. Their work has had a direct impact on my life and thus on many of the ideas presented in this book. I would highly recommend the following books to anyone in pursuit of self-knowledge:

Bach, Richard. *Illusions.* New York: Dell Publishing, 1977.

Bach, Richard. *Jonathan Livingston Seagull.* New York: The Macmillan Company, 1970.

Bradshaw, John. *Healing the Shame That Binds You.* Deerfield Beach, Florida: Health Communications Inc., 1988.

Chödrön, Pema. *When Things Fall Apart.* Boston: Shambhala Publications, 1997.

Epstein, Mark, M.D. *Going on Being.* New York: Broadway Books, 2001.

Epstein, Mark, M.D. *Going to Pieces Without Falling Apart.* New York: Broadway Books, 1998.

Epstein, Mark, M.D. *Thoughts Without a Thinker.* New York: Basic Books, 1995.

Gilbert, Roberta M., M.D. *Extraordinary Relationships.* New York: John Wiley & Sons Inc., 1992.

Miller, Alice. *The Drama of the Gifted Child.* New York: Basic Books, 1979, 1997.

Seigel, Daniel J. *The Developing Mind.* New York: The Guilford Press, 1999.

Tolle, Eckhart. *The Power of Now.* Novato, California: New World Library, 1999.

About the Author

Shannon Duncan began his efforts towards spiritual development and self-discovery at a very young age, and started working full time to help others in their personal and spiritual growth after retiring as an entrepreneur at the age of 29. He lives in San Diego, California, with his daughter. His website is www.shannonduncan.com..

Shannon has created a line of products,
including the Focus Tool,
developed specifically
to work synergistically with the concepts
in this book.
To learn more about them, visit:

www.pmasystem.com or www.audioserenity.com

or call toll free (866) 438-7626

New World Library is dedicated to
publishing books and audio products
that inspire and challenge us to improve
the quality of our lives and our world.

Our products are available
in bookstores everywhere.
For our catalog, please contact:

New World Library
14 Pamaron Way
Novato, California 94949

Phone: (415) 884-2100 or (800) 972-6657
Catalog requests: Ext. 50
Orders: Ext. 52
Fax: (415) 884-2199

Email: escort@newworldlibrary.com
Website: www.newworldlibrary.com